LOVE LIES

'Deborah McKinlay applies a scalpel to that delicate creature called Love – she makes you laugh while you wince with recognition'
Dr Maryon Tysoe

'A devastatingly truthful book which analyses the curious phenomenon we know as relationships'
Daily Mirror

'A witty round-up of all those familiar sayings and feelings we go through when we meet a man'
Today

'This guide through the minefield of relationships is a revelation for anyone who ever found themselves tearfully wondering What Went Wrong'
Sunday Independent

'True Lies, the truth about how men's minds really work'
Elle

'A minor classic'
South Wales Evening Post

Deborah McKinlay gives advice on sex to 720,000 men every month. As well as being *Esquire*'s agony aunt, she is a bestselling author. She lives a long way from anyone.

ALSO BY THE AUTHOR

Sex Secrets

Deborah McKinlay

LOVE LIES

What Men Don't Know
and Women Won't Admit

HarperCollins*Publishers*

HarperCollins*Publishers*
77–85 Fulham Palace Road,
Hammersmith, London W6 8JB

This paperback edition 1995
1 3 5 7 9 8 6 4 2

First published in Great Britain by
HarperCollins*Publishers* 1994

Copyright © Deborah McKinlay 1994

Illustrations by Josephine Sumner

The Author asserts the moral right to
be identified as the author of this work

ISBN 0 00638721 7

Set in Berkley Book

Printed in Great Britain by
HarperCollinsManufacturing Glasgow

Contents

If a Man begins to fall in love with a Woman
he doesn't call her for a bit.

If a Woman begins to fall in love with a Man
he doesn't call her for a bit.

If a Man doesn't call her for a bit, a Woman
can't decide whether to be nice to him when
he does call OR whether to give him a hard
time for not calling her for a bit.

A Man never understands why a Woman
gives him a hard time for NOT calling her
when he DOES call her.

1

It's Just a Phase

A woman knows the exact length of time it takes for a postcard to travel from anywhere in the world to her address.

A woman knows whether 'the phones were down'.

A woman's wardrobe is a testimony to the hobbies of her ex-lovers.

A woman KNOWS that 'I adore you' is NOT the same thing.

First Month Nausea is a female ailment. It is prevalent among women who are in Phase One of a new romance.

Men tend to forget that women can have their entire lives transformed as a result of a chance meeting in a bookshop. Women never forget this. If a woman meets Mr Right even her name can change. That is why women treat each new relationship with some degree of seriousness.

However, despite the fact that for a woman a 'new man' might mean a 'new life', it is men who make all the real decisions in the early stages. In the modern romance a woman gives a man the option to call her. Once she has given him this option, and he has given her the impression that it is one he'd like to act upon, they are in Phase One. She begins to wait and the longer she waits the worse her First Month Nausea condition gets.

PHASE ONE

Women stay in. In case he calls.
Women wonder if their answering machines are on the blink.
Women lift their telephone receivers to check for the dial tone.
Women create unspoken deadlines. He *has* to call by Day Three.
Women beat themselves up with little mental dialogues which go
something like this: 'I wish men wouldn't SAY they'd call. Why
do they say that? Why do I always go for unreliable bastards?
When did he say he was going to Vienna? Maybe he's already
gone. Maybe that's it . . . I wish I hadn't talked so much. I wish
I'd dressed more casually. Why do I always do this? Why do I
hang around . . . waiting? That's it. I'm NEVER doing this again.
He SEEMED so genuine. Maybe he called while I was at the
supermarket . . . maybe, maybe, maybe. . . '

Men change their lives in no way whatsoever.
Men are in a good mood because they've met a new woman who
seems quite fun and sexy.
Men eventually call, act flirty and casually suggest a rendezvous.
Men are blissfully unaware of the awesome significance of the
exact timing of their phone call.
Men unwittingly set Phase Two in motion.

PHASE TWO

Both sides are testing each other.
Both cautiously disclose a few selected facts about themselves.

He will, at least once, fail to call when he said he would.

She will, at least once, call him.

It should be noted that, though the 90s girl supposedly has the option of being the pursuer, EVERYONE knows it is not a real option. She *can* call but only in Phase Two and NEVER more than twice. Otherwise she is man-hungry, needy and maybe OBSESSIVE. Men and Women know this.

Even when the woman does exercise her Phase Two call option she usually needs fortifying by other women if not alcohol. When, with beating heart and trepidation, she finally dials his number she has another dilemma. He is not meant to be there. He is meant to be at his grandmother's funeral or out of town on urgent business. The hapless chap, quietly sitting at home watching TV and eating nacho chips, who answers the phone with a casual 'hello' to a woman who has been beating herself up for four days about his lack of calls has entered a minefield.

If favourable responses are encountered during Phase Two and the calls become slightly more frequent on his part, and *not at all* frequent on her part . . . If the sexual element of the relationship develops happily . . . AND if he gives in to his 'feel good' mood. . .

They will enter Phase Three.

PHASE THREE

He thinks, 'What the hell. She's great. Nice ass, nice eyes. Good sex.'

He calls her, a lot.

He just grins when friends suggest that there might be 'some woman'.

He tries not to think about her too much.

She tells her friends everything she knows about him and adds a few extra details for interest.

She will probably get a new haircut, lose weight and buy some new clothes.

She resents anything which stops her thinking about him.

Phase Three is lovely. It is the stage when both parties may consider themselves to be 'in love' (although men never use this phrase). They may say 'I love you'.

During Phase Three the 'feelings' of both people are very likely to be in sync. Their expectations and understanding of what these feelings mean, however, are probably completely different.

- A woman thinks that a man who is sleeping with her and has told her he loves her or even just behaved lovingly is faithful to her. The woman also thinks that under these circumstances the man should be faithful to her.

- A man in these circumstances hasn't given this issue any particular thought.

- A woman thinks that being faithful and being 'in love' means that the relationship has 'a future'.

- A man in these circumstances hasn't given this issue any particular thought.

- A woman wants to know what 'the future' is.

- A man in these circumstances has to think very fast.

It is not that men never want ongoing, monogamous relationships. Many do. It is just that they like to mull the idea over for a while, they like to muddle on with feeling good and having fun together. They like to 'see how things go'.

Women, though, like to 'know where they stand', and they like to know this very early on.

Actually, the woman would like to 'know where she stands' right from the first date, but she is aware that asking 'where she stands' so soon is likely to send Romeo running for cover. So she waits until she is over her First Month Nausea and when she figures that he is pretty keen she hits him with it. Hard.

The 'Where Do I Stand' Conversation

Points to Remember
The woman may be very indirect. She may begin by asking the man something like where he was on Thursday or whether he has seen his ex lately.

The woman has rehearsed this conversation. Possibly even with friends. Once she starts she cannot stop herself.

The woman waits until she feels sure of getting a good response from the man.

> **Which is why she always brings it up when they are having an otherwise terrific time.**

The man says nothing and tries to diffuse the little persistent, hinting queries with a hug.

She keeps at it.

The man becomes a bit irritated and says something like 'Let's not spoil things.'

She keeps at it.

The man gets angry and/or leaves.

She panics.

No man can ever begin to understand the level of panic a woman feels over a Phase Three row and exit. It consumes her.

Don't Forget. . .

She has spent every moment since she met the man considering the possibilities. Even if these musings have been idle. Even if she is intelligent and aware that 'it's too soon to tell'. She will have seriously considered that this man might be HIM. During Phase Three this feeling has gained ground rapidly.

She has talked endlessly about the man to her friends, often giving him qualities which he does not actually possess to make him seem like a real 'catch'.

This means that

1   She now believes in these qualities herself.
2   If she loses him it is doubly humiliating.

The woman reverts to Phase One. With a really bad case of First Month Nausea PLUS all the symptoms of a minor nervous breakdown.

The man feels a bit pissed off.

If the man has enough 'in love' feelings for the woman he will get around to calling her.

The man who makes this call . . . the man who sighs and figures that if he misses her this much then maybe there IS a future . . . the man who props his clay feet up on his desk at seven o'clock one evening and dials her number . . . has no idea of the level of responsibility he has just undertaken for another human being's happiness.

The woman who answers the phone (not before the third ring, please-please-please) and hears the longed for voice, IMMEDIATELY turns the owner of that voice into a GOD. The woman whose carefree tone completely belies her state of mind begins, from this moment, to pin her hopes and dreams on this man.

When these nervous breakdown stages in relationships are over, women refer to them as 'bad patches'. Men never refer to them at all

2

Going Public

Men know that they would be quite good at most things if they just had the time.

Many men think that they would be particularly good at Drumming or Playing a Bass Guitar. (Playing the Maracas is a lesser-known variant.)

During courtship they like to make the woman aware of this by giving her a quick demonstration of their 'drumming' or 'playing the bass guitar' style while they are dancing.

The woman is unimpressed but she knows this means he fancies her.

Other Things That Men Would Be Quite Good At:

- *Driving a racing car*
- *Flying a fighter jet*
- *Being a Fashion Photographer*

Things That Any Ponce Could Do:

- *Cook*
- *Write Poetry*

Women quite often need reminding of this.

If a man and a woman survive Phases One, Two and Three they become a 'couple'. Becoming a couple means that a woman can say, with some confidence, that a man is her 'boyfriend' and he will not deny it.

At this stage the relationship becomes a bit like a runaway train. The woman is in the engine room stoking the boiler as hard and fast as she can. The man is not too alarmed though, because he imagines that he is crawling along the top of the carriages like James Bond, and that it is only a matter of time before he coolly lowers himself through the appropriate aperture and takes control. For the time being he is just enjoying the adventure and the feel of the wind in his hair.

GOING PUBLIC RITUALS

The man and the woman introduce each other to their best friends.

When the woman meets the man's best friend she is concerned with:

1 Whether or not he has a girlfriend or wife.
2 Whether that girlfriend or wife is very pretty.
3 Whether he is faithful to that girlfriend or wife.
4 Whether he would like to find a girlfriend or wife if he doesn't have one.
5 Whether HE thinks that SHE will make a good girlfriend or wife.
6 Whether he will say this to HIM.

When the man meets the woman's best friend he is vaguely concerned with:

1 Whether or not she is fanciable.

> At this stage the couple may introduce each other to
> their families.
>   If they do meet, the woman is usually convinced that
> his family rather like her. The man is usually convinced
> that her family don't like him much.
>   Usually the reverse is true.

Between introductions the couple want to spend a lot of time
alone. This is the only time in a relationship when a woman
wants to sit on the sofa, eat pizza and watch TV with a man. A
man often makes the mistake of thinking that she will be happy
to go on sitting on the sofa, eating pizza and watching TV with
him.

**It is during this stage that the man begins to feel pretty
sure that his mere PRESENCE is enough to make this
woman happy.**

The woman, though, starts to get a teeny weeny bit bored with
this routine. Also, there isn't much to report back to the other
girls. She needs something a little more tangible to prove their
'coupledom'.

One night she suggests that she'd like to 'go away for the
weekend'.

The man doesn't mind this idea. Men generally don't mind
ideas which involve a beginning, a middle and an end.

Also, implicit in 'Going Away For the Weekend' is SEX.

As soon as the man has mumbled a half-enthusiastic consent into
her hair the woman jumps off the sofa and begins turning the
pages of *The Good Hotel Guide* with a speed and dexterity which
startles him.

Mentally, he leaps another carriage.

GOING AWAY FOR THE WEEKEND

The woman. . .
Has her hair cut. Has her bikini line waxed. Shaves her legs. Borrows a skirt from her best friend. Buys a new blouse. Dyes her eyelashes. Diets. Buys a new lipstick. Fills fifteen small plastic containers with lotion. Tries on all her clothes. Decides on 'the black'. Irons all her clothes. Packs most of her clothes. Packs something 'sexy'. Laughs about this with her friends. Tells everyone she knows that 'he is taking her away for the weekend'. Shows them the picture in *The Good Hotel Guide.*

The man. . .
Wonders if his wellies are in the car. Tells the other guy in the elevator that he reckons the A4 is a better bet on a Friday night.

The kind of hotel that new couples go to when they go away for the weekend attracts two sorts of clientele:

1 Other new couples who are going away for the weekend.
2 Couples who are on the first nights of their honeymoons.

The couples who are on the first nights of their honeymoons are glimpsed, only briefly, in the lobby. An unmarried woman, no matter how liberated, often feels a bit embarrassed at the check-in desk. Especially when she is with a new man and it is obvious to anyone that their suitcases are distinctly separate. So, when she sees the newlyweds she feels – just a teeny bit – jealous, of their easy togetherness. She buries this thought deep in her subconscious where it begins to take root.

11

When they get to their room, the man likes to have a quick tumble. The woman quite likes this too but she knows that it is not THE MAIN EVENT. She is looking forward to preparing for the main event. After the tumble she does this. Ostensibly she is getting ready for dinner. It takes a very long time.

The man would quite like a drink.

When the woman is ready (at just about the point when the man is considering going out to find a paper), they go down for dinner. They sit in the little bar drinking champagne cocktails and eating nuts. The man tells the woman she looks lovely. The woman smiles at him and fiddles with the stem of her champagne glass. She stops herself from throwing the nuts down her throat three at a time, the way she would if he wasn't there, and she has a little thought. It goes like this:

'IF he DID propose, I'd probably say yes. Probably. I wonder if we would live in his flat. No. We'd sell it and mine too and get something bigger. We could get something quite nice. We could get something with a garden. Something that would be big enough IF we DID have a child. I wouldn't go for all that white dress business, though. I'd want something a bit different.'

The man looks at her and thinks:
'Sweet . . . I wonder if this is the Tudor part of the building?'

The man says to the woman:
'I wonder if this is the Tudor part of the building?'

The woman feigns interest and smiles a little frozen smile. She keeps this smile glued on when the Patron comes over to ask if they'd like another champagne cocktail and her beloved asks him:
'Is this the Tudor part of the building?'
and what seems to her like an interminable conversation about this ensues.

They have a lovely dinner and laugh a lot.

Women quite like to talk about when they FIRST met. They like to create a history and, also, highlight the difference between those uncertain days and NOW.

Men are pretty hazy about the division, but they don't often tire of stories in which they are the hero.

Both are very happy and affectionate and probably a bit pissed by the time they wander, arm in arm, back to their room.

Now, more men than would care to admit it would quite happily forego the main event at this point, in favour of another brandy and eight hours sleep BUT women like to have a bit of passion to round off a romantic evening.

ALSO, the woman is prepared for this and has worn something under the new blouse to perk him up a bit.

Once they get going a pretty good time is had by both parties.

When the Passion is Spent

- The woman lies with her head on the man's chest tracing little circles on his body with her forefinger. She feels happy, loving, vulnerable, feminine and close to HIM.

- The man feels . . . hot.

- The woman LONGS for the man to say something to indicate that he feels happy, loving, vulnerable, masculine and close to HER.

- The man says, 'Do you find it stuffy in here?'

- The woman doesn't trust herself to speak, she makes a tiny shaking movement with her tousled head.

- The man gives her a little pat and then he gets out of bed and begins to fiddle with the window latch.

When the man has fiddled with the window latch to his heart's content and has created what he considers to be the perfect conditions for a good night's sleep, he goes to the bathroom to pee.

While the man is in the bathroom he pats, ineffectually, at his hair.

While the man is in the bathroom the woman brushes her hair, wipes the mascara off her cheeks, checks for smeared lipstick, rearranges herself and the bed and any items of clothing she might still be wearing so as to look completely alluring on his return.

The man returns, pats her again and indicates that, although he has NO INTENTION of sleeping for the rest of the night he WOULD like to sleep for a bit now. He puts his arm around her and dozes off. He feels very content.

The woman lies awake for quite a while. She feels very confused.

The next morning over breakfast she waits for a little indication of how the rest of the weekend will go.

The man asks her if she brought the map in from the car.

They are a couple.

3

Your Place or Mine

If a man points out some really gorgeous woman and says that he thinks she is attractive. . .
A woman feels a bit insecure.

If a man points out some dog ugly cow and says that he thinks she is attractive. . .
A woman feels worried.

If a man points out some really gorgeous woman and says that he doesn't think that she is attractive. . .
A woman says, 'Oh, Come ON!'

Sometimes, after a rather pleasant weekend away and a fairly spectacular main event, IF

1 The woman has not brought up the 'the future' conversation
2 The woman hasn't talked for the whole of the A4 traffic jam
3 The man doesn't have an early start on Monday

the idea of going back to their own houses is a bit depressing. So they don't.

They start 'living together'. Officially.

Usually before they begin 'living together officially' the woman has told people, 'We're not actually living together. I want to keep my independence till I'm SURE.' What this means is that she spends every minute of her free time with him. It means that she has most of her wardrobe in the boot of her car, in a carrier bag at her office and in a locker at the gym. It means that she went back to her flat last Friday when he was at some pre-arranged work thing. She spent the evening putting colour in her hair and wax on her legs.

If they have been spending most of their time at HER place he will have already moved most of his belongings and all of his clothes in. She has probably been laundering the latter with loving care and sighing over the former whenever he was at some pre-arranged work thing.

LIVING TOGETHER

- If they move into HER place, she IMMEDIATELY changes the message on the answering machine to a bubbly version which includes HIS name.
- She is surprised by how few things he's got. She is appalled by one particularly LARGE thing which he HAS got and wants to keep in the sitting room.
- She begins to feel that she can 'Be Herself'. She tells her friends how wonderful it is to be so relaxed with someone. She doesn't brush her hair any more while he is in the bath-room peeing, she doesn't shave her legs EVERY day, she starts wearing the underwear from the 'middle' drawer. She does these things because she trusts him. She trusts him because she loves him. She thinks he knows this.

- If they move into HIS place he resists any suggestion that they change the message on the machine. He mumbles some-thing about 'business calls'.
- He is horrified by how many things she's got. He makes a few rules about HIS DESK, HIS stereo and HIS GUITAR.

- He wonders why she hasn't worn that black thing for a few weeks.

Once a woman has presented herself to a man Mascara-less she feels pretty vulnerable. The newly 'living together' woman is just one fuzzy ball of LOVE. As she cooks his supper in her sarong and M&S vest she feels the 'couple cocoon' forming snugly around her.

Suddenly. . .

She is terrified of it going away. She dreads the thought of First Month Nausea or a Phase Three Walkout EVER happening again in her life. BUT she doesn't want to let on to HIM. She wants to be a bit of a cucumber so that he does not 'take her for granted'.

Given that:
a) She remembers the dire consequences of direct 'the future' enquiries
b) She doesn't want to seem needy, or OBSESSIVE
c) She has gotten this far

she swallows the fear.

The Insecurity Alien begins to come to life inside her

The woman doesn't usually realize that the best thing to do with an Insecurity Alien is to bludgeon, smother or starve it to death. The woman takes a feminine approach at first and tries to Pacify it.

She begins to hunt for little titbits of information which she can feed to the Insecurity Alien to keep it happy.

She does this by. . .
- Making little indirect jokes about 'the future'.
- Making little indirect jokes about 'the past'.
- Reminding HIM that she loves him, adores him, cares about him.
- Reminding her friends that he loves her, adores her, cares about her.

17

Unfortunately, the man responds with vague smiles and nods. So do her friends.

The Insecurity Alien begins to kick. This is when the woman remembers THE BOX.

No matter whose house they are living in, the woman is intrigued by a small box full of correspondence which the man dumps, nonchalantly, next to his sports bag.

Within easy view . . . almost.

Within easy reach . . . certainly

Now, it is not that women do not have boxes of correspondence *but* if they move in with a man they may leave this at their sister's house, they may put it in the bottom of a suitcase. They may even, in a flush of optimism about 'the future', chuck it. What they do not do is leave this box within easy view and even easier reach of their new *enamorato*. That would be asking for trouble, wouldn't it? Well, wouldn't it?

In the first weeks after the man and woman have moved in together the woman is very cool about THE BOX. At first she just dusts the box and wonders. She doesn't SNOOP.

Men tend to be under a misapprehension about women snooping.

Men think that women do it because they are unfailingly nosy. This is only partly true.

A woman snoops because she feels vulnerable.

ALSO, men make it easy.

On the day when the woman watches her hand reach out, of its own volition, and tentatively remove an envelope from the box, her heart is beating wildly.

Now,

1 Men tend to be sentimental which means that they keep lots of little insignificant notes and bits of nonsense.
2 Men may keep these little notes and bits of nonsense in the same box as their tax return and a three-year-old power bill.

The initial foray reveals this, BUT the woman who is carrying a first-trimester Insecurity Alien does not heave a sigh of relief and continue dusting the box. She digs.

A woman on a serious SNOOP is an awesome thing. She can't stop.

She ALWAYS finds SOMETHING.

Things That Newly Living Together Snooping Women Find . . .

- A card, inscribed with a cryptic message in a feminine hand. (The postmark is four years old.)
- An old photograph of HIM. He has his arm around another woman and he looks perfectly happy about it.
- An earring.

It's not that women don't understand that a man has a past. It is just that Phases One, Two and Three help her to forget.

In fact, the woman, *can* deal with 'the past'. *If* she can isolate it from 'the present' and 'the future'. But, this is hard for her.

She thinks: If he was happy before, maybe he can be happy again.

Without me.

Women tend to imagine that they were never REALLY happy before THIS man came along.

The greatest praise a woman can give a new relationship is IT'S DIFFERENT.

This means 'better'. This means everything before must have been lousy. Doesn't it? Well, doesn't it?

The woman now has 'evidence' of a happy past.
The woman is not stupid.
The woman knows that she cannot confront the man with this.
The woman knows that she cannot confess her fears to her friends.
The woman knows that this is 'just silly'.

The Insecurity Alien is growing and growing.
   Hinting has failed, Snooping has failed.
   She tries CONSOLIDATING.

Consolidating Tactics

- Making herself domestically indispensable.
- Making herself KNOWN at his workplace.
- Reminding him of her devotion by sending him love notes and phoning him.
- Planning. Outings, treats, holidays.
- Doing Everything with HIM.

Modern women do not just turn into *hausfraus* overnight. Modern women keep up their girls' nights and aerobics classes. What modern women NEVER admit is that they arrange these activities AROUND the man. They do these things when he is at some pre-arranged work thing.

The man begins, slowly, to sense an undercurrent. He can't put his finger on exactly *what* is going on, but he has a growing feeling of UNEASE. He gets a bit squirmy. He feels a teeny bit *trapped*.

HE BREAKS OUT.

The man isn't even all that sure that he *is* breaking out. He still loves the woman. He rather enjoys having fresh pasta cooked for him occasionally. He has clean shirts. He likes his presents. He doesn't mind the treats and outings. It's just . . . something.

One day the girl in the photograph rings him, out of the blue, and he hears himself suggesting, or even just agreeing to, LUNCH.

He doesn't mention this at home.

The woman. . .
Feels her antennae twitching madly. She figures that this time there really is something up. She makes a HUGE effort and plans a wonderful week-end for them. By Sunday evening she feels MUCH Better. As she sits on the sofa, eating pizza and watching TV with him, just like the old days, she thinks, 'It's all right. Silly me.'

The man. . .
Begins to relax, cautiously at first, but by Sunday night when they are sitting on the sofa, eating pizza and watching TV just like the old days, he thinks, 'This is silly.'
He tells her.

The man does not tell the woman everything. He only tells her about the phone call.

21

Love Lies

The woman doesn't need to be told. She already KNOWS.

The woman gives birth to a full-term Insecurity Alien. Right there in the sitting room. The agony of doing this etches deep lines on her face. Her voice rises to screaming pitch.

The man is appalled, horrified, terrified. He runs like hell.

The woman is exhausted. She collapses.

When the man stops running he has a bit of a think.

This is what he thinks: 'She must REALLY love me.'

The man goes home. When he gets there the woman is wearing her sarong and M&S vest. She isn't wearing any mascara. She looks like a fuzzy ball of LOVE.

The man gives her a big kiss.

They say 'I love you.'

The woman . . . wonders where he's been.

4

The Battle

A woman has a small part in her brain (about the size of a green pea) which Understands that a man who is standing in a room full of business colleagues is NOT likely to say 'I love you too, Bubba, BIG kiss,' over the phone.

The rest of her goes into a bit of a huff.

When a man is a boy-child he does something like this:

a) Shoots a bird with an air gun.
b) Puts the family dog in a box and beats the box with a big stick.
c) Tortures a kitten with a firecracker.

The boy-child feels pretty lousy about this. He carries around the burden of his guilt for a long time. Then he grows up and gets a girlfriend and he tells her all about it.

The girlfriend thinks that this story, and the fact that the man has told it to her, is evidence of his vulnerability, openness and love.

She does not see it for what it is. A CAUTIONARY TALE.

One day, when the girlfriend is being fragile like the little bird, pesky like the wee kitten and doe-eyed and devoted like the family dog, the man takes out his air gun and shoots her.

As the woman lies wounded, weeping and wondering how someone she loves SO MUCH could be SO CRUEL to her, she STILL doesn't make the connection.

IN THE TRENCHES

The woman. . .
Gets over her insecurity problem. She feels pretty OK about the man coming back if she should lapse just slightly. She acts sweet and docile. She is happy to go to work, come home, have the odd drink with the girls and wake up next to HIM. She feels all safe and calm inside. She is the envy of her friends.

The man. . .
Feels a bit edgy. He is convinced of her total devotion. He notices that her legs get downright scratchy these days. He notices that she is always wearing that vest. He notices that she is always there.

The fuzzy ball of love begins to look a bit ragged round the edges.

He alternates between pissed offedness and guilt.

She starts making little hints about dinners and flowers and presents. This really gets him. He begins to feel that he has been HAD. This woman led him to believe that:

1 She was an undemanding sex machine.
2 She was happy just to be near him.

Now she wants Valentines and cards and flowers for no particular reason. This man considers himself nagged. This man wants a 'night off'.

The 'night off' is the death knell for the woman's calm feeling. She has a bit of a think. This is what she thinks:

'I mustn't panic. I mustn't start being insecure. I mustn't let him see that I am feeling insecure. I must seem relaxed about this. I must give him some space. I'll organize a girls' night.'

She organizes the girls' night. She carries it off with aplomb. She impresses the other girls with her casual attitude. She makes it clear that their relationship is solid enough for them to 'do their own thing'.

A girls' night is when more than two women get together and drink a bit and EAT A LOT.

Gluttony is the glue of sisterhood.

Women like to eat far more than they ever let on to men. They also like to talk dirty and laugh guttural laughs. Most men would feel very threatened if they found themselves unprotected in the midst of a full-throttle girls' night.

After the girls have gone, she puts on the 'black thing' and waits . . . and waits. No matter how late he is, no matter how little interest he shows in her attire, she does not say one word. In the morning she says, 'Have a good time, Sweetie?' This is the extent of her enquiry.

The man looks up at her. Loyal, loving, TRYING really hard, and he says, 'Do you have to know EVERYTHING? Can't I have ONE night out? Can't I do any bloody thing without you needing to know all about it?' and leaves for work.

The Battle Rages

The woman takes a totally defensive stance. She grits her teeth and holds on. When she can no longer hide the evidence of her tears, she tells friends that they are having a bit of a 'bad patch'.

The man cannot control the boy-child. He is almost compulsive in his cruelty. This woman just will not fight back. He hits her a bit harder. He can't help himself. He just wants to see how much this poor, dumb animal will take.

When the man finally looks up and sees the blood staining the white feathers of the little bird's chest, when he stops shouting and hears the yelps of his devoted canine companion, when he holds still for a moment and feels the wee kitten brushing up against his legs. . .
He feels like hell.

In the heat of the battle the man will have:

- Not returned her calls to the office.
- Told her she doesn't know a THING about something.
- Come home late when she has invited another couple for supper.
- Gone away for a weekend without her.
- Let her go to her Mother's birthday party or her best friend's wedding on her own.

The woman will have:

- Smiled.
- Cried.
- Made Excuses.

There is one other thing that the woman does. She remembers.

When it is All Over. . .

The man thinks it is all over.

The woman thinks: 'Next time he is not going to get away with it.'

5

Who's a
Naughty Boy Then?

....

*A woman is never quite sure whether her boyfriend could be a:
Commitment-Phobic, Most Likely to Stray, Hooked on Pseudo
Intimacy , Go-Away Come-Closer Man posing as an ordinary bloke.
She finds it useful to do a bit of reading up on this just to be sure.*

WOMEN'S MAGAZINES KNOW THIS.

....

After the battle, the woman likes to lick her wounds for a bit and
the man likes to assuage his guilt. So. . .
   He takes her out for dinner.
   Buys her a present.
   Maybe takes her away for the weekend.

And. . .
She lets him.

A subtle shift begins in the balance of power. The woman has
learned two things:

1 He is not a god.
2 He did not leave.

They settle into a cosy routine. They compromise a bit. She no longer organizes everything around him. He checks with her when he is arranging a 'night off'.

Men's nights off take all sorts of guises. They may involve elaborate props like squash courts, golf clubs, old school friends or even clients.

Sometimes they get straight to the point and just go to the pub.

NIGHT-OFF RITUALS

Some men do talk about women on their nights off, they talk like this:

'Diane all right?'

'Fine . . . Kate?'

'Fine.'

Pause.

'See that Karen in Accounts?'

'Yeah.'

'Tits on her.'

'Yeah.'

Chuckles. Pause.

'See the match?'

'Whooaa, that last goal!'

Animated conversation.

A man who is just a teeny bit later than he said he would be on his night off says, 'I'm really going to be in the doghouse now.'

When the Man Gets Home Just a Teeny Bit Later than He Said He Would. . .

The landing light is not glowing a cheery welcome. It is very dark. This means he has a spot of trouble getting his key in the lock.

Once he is safely inside, he heads for the kitchen. He opens and closes all the cupboards and runs the cold tap on full pressure for several minutes. Then he suddenly thinks of something. It is something that he needs to FIND.

Now, this something could be his first Boy Scout badge or it could be a report that he needs for a meeting the following day. Whatever it is, it is extremely important that he locates this thing. NOW.

When the Man Gets Home Four Hours Later than He Said He Would. . .

The woman wakes up with a start. She has only just fallen into a deep sleep after having lain awake for the first 'hour late', fumed for the second 'hour late', fretted for the third 'hour late'. At the end of the third hour she gave up fretting, had a brief reversal to fuming and got up to turn off the landing light.

When she hears the man in the kitchen she feels relief and irritation in equal measure. She feigns sleep. She keeps feigning sleep for several minutes in anticipation of his guilty creep into the bedroom. She waits. She considers whether or not she'll give him a cuddle when he does his guilty clamber into bed. She decides maybe. She waits. She thinks, 'What on EARTH is he doing?' She waits. She gets really mad. She gets up and staggers out of the bedroom.

She sees the man sitting cross-legged on the floor with the contents of two drawers and several cupboards spread out around him. She flips. She says: 'You are not the only person who lives here, you know. I've got an important meeting in the morning and I would like to get some sleep. You are SO selfish.'

She thinks: 'Now I'm going to have PUFFY EYES.'

The man thinks: 'I'm really in the doghouse now.'

The next morning the man knows that he is in the doghouse because the woman talks to him in a little, strangled, clipped kind of a voice. She looks quite grumpy and she has puffy eyes. If he tries to give her a bit of a smooch (just to test the water), she is fairly offhand.

They go to work. By the time six o'clock rolls around the man is feeling pretty grim. He needs a quiet night. He cannot face the thought of a telling off. He cannot face the thought of being in the doghouse. He searches his foggy brain for some original and clever scheme which will alleviate this problem.

He thinks: 'I know, I'll give her some flowers.'

Giving her some flowers

Men think that. . .

1 It is pretty dense that women like getting flowers.
2 Giving flowers is a bit of a waste of money but women like it.
3 Flowers are a kind of cure-all panacea to women. (This is partly true.)
4 It is the thought that counts. (This is completely untrue.)

WOMEN AND FLOWERS: THE FACTS

If a woman receives one dozen long-stemmed yellow roses in a box tied with a silk ribbon at her office. . .

She does not care if his secretary called the florist.

'At the office' is key. Whenever a florist's delivery arrives 'at the office', all the females on the premises think, 'Me me me ooh please me . . . lucky cow.'

They say, 'Aren't they GORGEOUS, lucky you. Isn't he a GOOD boy!'

The woman carries these flowers home on the bus like a trophy. She thinks: 'He is a good boy really.'

(When a woman sees another woman carrying home a trophy bunch of flowers, she thinks, '*She's* not that pretty . . . she must have left her job.' She is green with envy.)

The man who spends forty-five minutes in the rush hour trying to find a grocer's which sells flowers and then comes home, hopefully, clutching a damp bunch of carnations (which he has paid over the odds for), is likely to see this same bunch of carnations languishing in the kitchen sink the next morning.

On Valentine's Day there is always a pretty girl on the train with a good body, long hair and a short skirt. She is carrying masses of flowers and little coloured boxes.

The other women on the train think: 'Why DO men always go for that type?'

Between minor misdeeds and make-ups the couple go along like this:

The woman. . .
Does most of the housework. Pays her half of holidays and treats. Saves up for his Christmas present. Buys the groceries. Cleans the loo. Watches James Bond videos with him. Watches car racing with him. Nags a bit. Drops off his dry-cleaning. Calls the Gas Board. Waits for the man from the Gas Board. Buys a new duvet cover. Buys a Le Creuset casserole dish. Does most of the cooking. Feels married. Nags a bit. Thinks, we may as well BE married.

The man. . .
Cooks spag bol, occasionally. Agrees to go to a Merchant Ivory film, once in a blue moon. Wonders what to do with his bonus. Never thinks about marriage.

One day when the woman is waiting for the Gas Board chap, she decides to get out the man's blue suit. She intends to drop it off at the dry cleaner's on her way to the office. In the course of clearing out the pockets she comes across something. Something that brings back a lot of buried and – she'd hoped – dead emotions.

Things Women Find in Suits They're Taking to the Dry Cleaner's . . .

a) A piece of message paper with 'Nicky called' written on it.
b) A flip-top matchbox from an expensive restaurant.
c) A petrol receipt from an out-of-town garage.

None of these things are, in themselves, incriminating. . .
    But they are SUSPICIOUS.

The woman decides that, under these circumstances, a SNOOP is called for.

This SNOOP bears no resemblance to her earlier fumbling attempts.

This SNOOP requires surgical gloves and a scalpel.

The woman sets about it. She is a woman with a mission.

That night when six o'clock rolls around, the man is feeling pretty OK. He stops at the grocer's on the way home and buys the ingredients for his 'special' recipe spag bol.

As he opens the front door he hums a little tune. . .

6

Ain't Misbehavin'

A man is perfectly capable of bringing a woman's menstrual cycle into an argument if he senses that he is losing ground.

A chap has a few stock phrases which he finds useful when it comes to dealing with women. They go like this:

- I didn't want to hurt you.
- I thought it was what you wanted.
- I'm here, aren't I?
- I didn't plan this. (Variant – It just happened.)

When a man is faced with a woman with narrowed eyes and flaring nostrils, he stands his ground for a moment. In fact, the man may continue to whistle and saunter about for a bit in the hope that he is misreading the signals. Even when the woman actually starts pawing the ground, the man simply steels himself for the first assault. He doesn't want to waste one of these little gems before it is absolutely necessary.

Also, he needs to know:

1 How serious the attack will be.
2 What *particular* thing triggered it off.

THE CIRCUMSTANCES UNDER WHICH A WOMAN WILL ATTACK

The woman prefers to attack when she has enough evidence to justify a good head of steam and, hopefully, a grovelling apology and improved behaviour from him.

So, if she has corroborative clues, for example:

- a business card which says 'Jennie's Jewels'
- a packet of girl-type cigarettes
- a second piece of message paper with what looks like '—cky called' written on it

she will go for it.

But. . .

If an unmarried, in-love woman finds feminine underwear in her boyfriend's car or a letter which says 'I love you too', she may just throw up, cry, put the underwear and letter back EXACTLY where she found them, take a bath and cook HIS favourite supper.

> **Whether or not she decides to confront the man at this stage, the woman will begin to SNOOP as a matter of course. From this point on the woman knows EVERY move the man makes. She will ALWAYS know when he is lying to her.**

THE ATTACK

The woman has been building up to the attack all day. This means that she tends to use up most of her energy on the first charge.

The man is not in doubt for very long as to PRECISELY what he is in trouble for. He only really listens to her first sentence, after that he begins to think about which defence best suits the situation.

The woman makes all her accusations (plus a few extras for good measure) and displays all her 'evidence'. When she has done this she stands back and glares at him. She feels triumphant, self-righteous and relieved. She waits for him to explain (and maybe beg forgiveness).

The man says: 'I can't believe you SNOOPED.'

This THROWS the woman. She has spent the day working herself into a frenzy over her 'in the rightness' and his 'in the wrongness' and now *she's* being accused.

She says: 'I didn't.' She knows that this is a bit lame. 'I was just. . .' she knows that she is losing ground '. . . if you took your OWN suit to the drycleaners. . .' This gets her back on to the attack. She feels a bit better. She adds a few complaints about having to do everything for him and having to hang around for the gas man.

The man senses his advantage. As long as she's in general nag mode he can deal with her. He is keen to keep her off specifics for as long as possible.

He says something like 'Oh, here we go. . .'

This leads them into a full-scale barney that rages inconclusively for quite a while until the woman suddenly remembers and confronts him all over again with THE EVIDENCE.

The man pauses for a moment, sighs and then tells her in a reasoning, 'this is just silly' tone about some woman who is, you know, a bit keen on him.

He hasn't told her about it before because he didn't want THIS to happen. He hasn't told the keen woman where to get off because 'he doesn't like hurting people'. He didn't 'plan' to have dinner with her. 'It just happened.' It means nothing to him. Would he be HERE if it did? . . . And as to her having to do things for him well he's sorry. Really he is. He thought it was what SHE wanted.

He gives her a bit of a hug. She has a bit of a sniffle.

He says he WAS going to cook her his special recipe spag bol. She wishes she could turn the clock back. She offers to make him his favourite supper.

He says no, it's too late now. They'll have pizza and HE'LL go out for it.

While the man is out getting the pizza (it takes a while), he thinks, 'Close.'

While the man is out getting the pizza, the woman thinks, 'Oh God, I feel such a fool. I wish I hadn't said anything. We could have had a really nice evening. Oh well. I'll be really sweet to him when he gets back. I won't say another word. Not ONE word. I am not going to be POSSESSIVE. If I'm really cool about this it'll all be OK. We'll just forget about it.'

It is quite late by the time they've had their pizza.

The woman is just as sweet as pie and makes lots of idle chatter about this and that to the man.

The man smiles and nods and then makes it clear that he'd like a cuddle and that she shouldn't fuss with the cleaning up.

The woman smiles and nods.

Later on she starts thinking about how awful the kitchen is going to smell if she doesn't throw away the pizza box so she offers to get some water and has a bit of a tidy up in the kitchen while she's about it.

On the way back to the bedroom she sees the man's jacket over the back of a chair. She fights a tiny little curious urge.

When she gets back into bed, the man says 'Thanks, Sweetie' for his water. He puts his arm around her and falls asleep. He has the cutest hint of a smile on his boyish features.

The woman strokes him absent-mindedly. She looks at his face. She thinks about his jacket. She remembers First Month Nausea. She looks at his face. She goes over his story. She thinks about his jacket. She looks at his face. She thinks of . . . a crocodile.

7

The Thrill Has Gone

••

Girl-Talking

'You know how I can never get our cleaner to change the sheets?'
'Yeah. . . ?'
'I'm always *having* to leave notes saying PLEASE change the sheets.'
'Right.'
'Well, when I went away last week I didn't leave a note.'
'Uh huh.'
'The sheets were changed.'
Thoughtful pause.
'What d'you think?'
Forty-five-minute analysis ensues.

••

Sometimes a woman finds stuff when she's snooping that really gets her down. Sometimes a woman gets tired of waiting for the gas man. Sometimes a woman in these circumstances begins to think that maybe she should just 'leave him'. All women SAY that 'in these circumstances' they definitely would leave him. Somehow, though, the woman feels that if she just leaves him, without a fight, he will have 'gotten away with it'.

Also, she still 'loves' him.

Nevertheless, she begins to have vague fantasies about a garden flat and maybe a kitten. She thinks how it might be quite fun to have HER friends over whenever she wants. She thinks these things when she is on her way to work and she is late after going via the dry cleaner's. They are vague musings and she does NOT mention them to him.

A woman who is thinking along these lines can really make a man's life a misery. She starts a little campaign . . . just to let him know that she is 'on to' him and that he is not going to get away with it.

WHAT A WOMAN DOES WHEN SHE IS VAGUELY THINKING OF LEAVING A MAN

- Gets all her hair cut off. (When the man says, 'But I loved your hair,' she says, ' You are *such* a sexist. You think all women should have long hair and short skirts.')
- Flirts dangerously with his best friend. (When the man sulks about this she says, 'What's the matter with you NOW?')
- Acts incredibly cheerful and good moodish in public and incredibly sullen and bad moodish in private.
- Stiffens whenever the man touches her.
- Goes out late with her friends and comes home looking a bit the worse for wear and mysterious.
- Sighs a lot and rolls her eyes whenever the man says anything.
- Accidentally tapes over his James Bond videos.

After quite a lot of this the man says something like 'Look, I think I'll go and stay with Jimbo for a bit.'

The woman weeps bitter tears and says, 'How could you do this to me?'

> No matter what the circumstances of a break-up, in her heart of hearts a woman always considers that she has been DUMPED.

When a man goes 'to stay with Jimbo for a bit', he isn't actually leaving. The woman may suspect that he is trying to. Her friends will definitely suspect this. But the man thinks that he is just 'going to stay with Jimbo for a bit'.

A man doesn't like to burn his bridges.

The man thinks that if he goes to stay with Jimbo for a bit. . .

1 He can misbehave whenever he wants to (without hurting anybody).
2 He can come home whenever he wants to.

The man only packs a very small bag.

The woman cries a bit less when she notices this.

The man suggests that she might want to come with him to Jimbo's, they could go out for a pasta when he's dropped his bag off.

At first the woman can't face this idea but eventually she goes with him. She can't bear the thought of having supper without him.

The woman can't eat her pasta.

The man says, 'I've always liked the pasta here.'

The woman cannot imagine how he can say something like *that* at a time like *this*. She starts to feel weepy all over again. She starts to get weepy all over again.

The man thinks, 'Oh, Hell'. He suggests that she comes back to Jimbo's. At first the woman can't face this idea but eventually she goes with him. She can't bear the thought of spending the night without him. She sleeps with him on the sofa bed in Jimbo's spare room.

In the morning the woman goes home. She is looking forward to having a proper bath because there were no dry towels at Jimbo's place. She thinks vague thoughts of garden flats and kittens.

The woman spends the first few weeks of their separation telling her friends that it is just a bad patch and that they have decided to spend some time apart. She makes it clear that this decision is mutual. At night she fights the urge to call him, rediscovers First Month Nausea symptoms and cries herself to sleep because he's 'left her'.

One evening (at about the point where the woman has stopped crying herself to sleep), the man calls her. He tells her how much he misses her. He says he'd really like to see her tonight. It's Phase Three all over again.

The woman. . .
Shaves her legs. Washes her hair. Puts clean sheets on the bed. (NOT that she's going to LET him stay.) Does her make-up. Decides what to wear. Changes her mind. Re-does her make-up. Puts on nice underwear. (NOT that she's going to LET him see it.) Wonders where he'll take her for dinner. Thinks, 'He did mean dinner?' Thinks, 'Of course he did.' Thinks, 'If he thinks I'm going to LET him. . .' Checks the fridge for pâté. Gets dressed. Waits. . .

The man. . .
Stops for a bottle of wine on the way.

When the doorbell goes the woman's heart skips a beat.

Much later, after they have drunk the wine and she has LET him, when he is scouring the fridge for pâté, she wonders if she's done the right thing. She wonders if this means that he's coming back. She thinks, 'If he does come back at least I'll know where I stand.'

The man thinks how nice it is to find pâté in the fridge and dry towels in the bathroom. He thinks that it is nice to see the old girl again too. He thinks, 'I might move back in for a bit. We'll see how things go.'

8

Make or Break

A woman can eat a plate of buffet food, balance a glass of wine, carry on a conversation with several people AND clock three seconds of eye contact between Her man and some blonde on the other side of the room.

If the man is damn fool enough to laugh during this exchange he will be under strict surveillance for the rest of the evening.

The man is blissfully unaware of this.

When they get in the car to go home, the man notices that the woman is a bit quiet.

He says, tentatively, '. . . Good party.'

She says, 'Well, YOU certainly seemed to enjoy yourself.'

If a couple give things 'another go' AND

- She still hates the way he holds his knife
- He stops trying to give her a smooch

. . . they break up.

When a Couple Breaks Up

A woman. . .
- Is devastated
- Cries a lot
- Loses weight
- Hates HIM
- Loves HIM
- Hates HIM
- Doesn't get a new boyfriend for ages
- Eventually gets over it

A man. . .
- Feels pretty low
- Gets a new girlfriend in about two weeks
- Thinks fondly about HER
- Never quite gets over it

But. . .
If She finds it kind of touching that he holds his knife like a pen and He persists in giving her a smooch, quite often they become a long-term thing. Couples can go on breaking up and making up for ages because of Slushy Love Gum.

EXAMPLES OF SLUSHY LOVE GUM

A framed snapshot of the two of them on holiday looking radiantly happy and 'in love'.

A VERY late-night conversation they had VERY early on during which they decided that if they had a son they'd call him 'Sebastiano'.

The man likes the woman's bottom.
The woman likes the man's bottom.

The special delivery toy robot which the woman sent to the man once for no reason at all.

The 'surprise' weekend in Paris.

Their restaurant.

Something that made them laugh so much they had to leave the restaurant.

Her name for him. His name for her.

> Slushy Love Gum does dissolve somewhat with time but, generally, a bit of it sticks and can only be removed by persistent chipping.

Slushy Love Gum is the tie that binds and it can hold a couple together for a very, very, very long time. It certainly seems like a very, very, very long time to His Mother. One day His Mother says something like:

'So, when are you two going to put us all out of our misery, then? We could do with a nice wedding before we're too old to enjoy it.'

(Her Mother said something like this to Her when they first started 'Living Together'. She hasn't bothered since.)

When His Mother says this the woman stops helping to dish up the roast potatoes for a mega second and then smiles an embarrassed, tight little smile and looks at Him . . . for a mega second. Then she gives His Father some more roast potatoes.

The man says something like:

'Good God, Ma, give us a break. IF we decide to get married it'll be when WE are ready. Anyway, we're perfectly happy as we are. Aren't we, Poppet?'

Poppet smiles the little, embarrassed, tight smile again and takes the potato dish out to the kitchen.

The thing is that the woman has been going along just fine for quite a while. Ever since he came back from Jimbo's she's felt pretty OK. She's been able to say to her friends, with some degree of honesty. . .

'I'm really happy with the way things are now. Eventually we'll probably get married, because, you know, we'd BOTH like to have kids SOME day, but for now. . .'

Essentially the woman thinks the same as the man. They ARE happy as they are and it is THEIR decision. The problem is the *IF*.

When they are driving home in the car this *IF* hangs in the air between them. It is engulfed in a huge, grey cloud. It stops them from talking very much. The *IF* cloud condenses and begins to rain little spots, just little ones, but they leave puddles.

That night she goes to bed quite early and he sits up for a bit. They both feel the damp.

A man and a woman who have gotten to the stage where *IF* is even an issue are probably good friends.

The woman says proudly: 'We're each other's BEST friends.'

A man says: 'I suppose we're sort of friends really.'

> A woman considers that being Best Friends is a key element of Slushy Love Gum.
>
> A man considers that being Best Friends *might* mean that he isn't a thing of beauty and a boy for ever.

Low Pressure is building.

The woman in an *IF* cloud has a dilemma. The Modern Girl can't issue an Ultimatum.

1 It is too uncool.
2 She might get Dumped.

She decides to show the man how much nicer his life would be if she were his wife.

She does this by acting as if she were ALREADY his wife.

The man: Misbehaves.

The man's misbehaviour is not like the naughty flirtations he has dallied with previously. The man goes out with the absolute intention of pulling . . . seriously. (Later he denies this to both women.)

The man needs to know two things:

1 Can he still?
2 Does he want to still?

He thinks that this will answer the *IF* question.

The woman considers her 'investment' in the relationship. The woman decides the time has come for her to get a return on this investment.

No matter how many storms the man creates she remains cool.

Ice begins to form on the puddles.

9

Slug It Out

A woman thinks that if she can just get a man AWAY from everything (Work/Hobby/Wife/Mistress/Mother) he will suddenly look at her and be AWARE of her wonderfulness. She thinks that if she can get him alone on a remote beach with NO distractions he may even talk about his FEELINGS.

If the man agrees to go to a remote beach with her she packs two large, soft bags full of 'capsule wardrobe' outfits and lots of beauty products made out of fruit.

The man packs some trunks, a polo shirt and a hat.

When they get to the beach the man is tetchy because the woman spends the whole time wearing his polo shirt and hat.

The woman sulks because the man always manages to find something to DO, he never talks about his feelings and he gripes at her for wearing his stupid hat.

There comes a point in the long-term relationship when the Man knows that what he would most like is for the Woman to disappear, in a quiet and unobtrusive manner. She should leave behind a half bottle of nail polish or some other gentle, distinctly feminine fingerprint for him to get slightly nostalgic over (and the new girlfriend to get hysterical over) and a note. The note should imply that even though she knows this is for the best, she'll never feel about anyone else the way she did about him and that, if he should find himself alone and a bit pissed and musing on the good times at four a.m. some New Year's Eve, it would be OK to call her.

Now, there are two major obstacles to this plan:

1   Men are too gutless to actually tell women this. They prefer to allow a row about where the car is parked to escalate to the stage where they shout, 'I don't know why we're still together anyway' . . . women ignore this – 'It was a silly fight about where we parked the car.'
2   Women have an in-built radar to rival bats when it comes to sensing potential break-up territory. This is a game they know. This is Slug It Out. No man has the stamina of a woman when it comes to the Slug It Out game.

HOW TO PLAY SLUG IT OUT

SHE. . .
Begins to ignore even the most obvious clues of his misbehaviour.
Acts sweet and sexy.
Calls him by his pet name.
Cooks his breakfast.

HE. . .
Feels a bit baffled.

SHE. . .
Buys him something that she knows he's been hankering for and he knows she can't afford.
Does not ask him why he was late or query the unfamiliar phone number which popped up on the last itemized bill.
Remembers his mother's birthday.

HE. . .
Feels a bit baffled and a bit guilty.
Then: Feels quite affectionate and sentimental about her.

SHE. . .
Brings up the 'the future' conversation.

HE. . .
Feels trapped.
Then: Acts Panicky.

SHE. . .
Cries. A lot.

IMPASSE.

When they reach the crying a lot impasse, the man reverts quickly to misbehaving and the woman reverts double quickly to stage one of Slug It Out and they start all over again.

The thing about Slug It Out is that it can go on for an age. If women decide to play for a wedding ring they can keep it up till hell freezes over.

A woman knows that men are

1 Sentimental
2 Solution-Orientated
3 Lazy

These traits mean that Slug It Out often gets results in the end. Given that a man never gets to go to bed with a woman and wake up with a note, given that he is genuinely nostalgic about the good times, given that leaving himself would involve major effort, given that he just wants the crying to STOP . . . The man may relent. The man may propose.

WOMEN KNOW THIS.

Slug It Out Variations

Some men are familiar with Slug It Out tactics. These men are, typically, of the over forty, playboy heart-throb or married-before variety. When these men feel a Slug It Out bout coming on they smile to themselves as they are eating their cooked breakfast and think:

'Not me sweetheart.'

This man told this woman on date two:

'Hey, I'm not marrying ANYBODY.'

He thought that by saying this he had made himself clear, given himself a get-out.

This man does not realize that the woman who has kept her cool and hung in, despite this warning, is probably a master player too. The woman who has spent a few years with a non-committer is usually a perfect judge of his panic points. She uses this skill to create a Slug It Out game which is so complexly plotted, so full of exquisite moves and countermoves, that he hardly knows he's playing. When Slug It Out becomes a psychological thriller, a woman can stay ahead of the game for a good long time. The man may relent. The man may propose.

The 'Other Woman' Exit Card

If a man really wants OUT, he will play a few rounds but then he might bring in reinforcements. He may opt to play the 'other woman' exit card. This is a tough one. The man considers it only as a last resort. The problem is that the woman does not give him the option of subtlety. The man would prefer to leave a few clues around, face up to one last, major crying bout and then be left to a life of simple bachelorhood and fun times. The woman who is playing Slug It Out ignores this. The man has to become more and more obvious. This gives him a double dilemma.

1   The final move is going to have to be HIS. He hates this.

2   The other woman becomes increasingly confident and starts to prepare herself for taking over the role of incumbent. He hates this.

Then there is the awful realization that Everyone is going to call him a bastard. The woman can stay ahead of THIS game for a good long time. The man may relent. The man may propose.

The FINAL solution

Sometimes a woman wakes up after a particularly bad crying bout, stumbles into the bathroom to pee and catches sight of herself in the mirror. The face which stares back at her is a grim reminder of Slug It Out's awful legacy. She stares at this face for a while and is able, vividly, to picture the deep furrows that have lined it for days. She hears herself begging, pleading, whining and cajoling and she is appalled. This woman may just walk back into the bedroom and pack a bag. This woman is all cried out. This woman throws in the towel.

The funny thing is that after she throws in the towel, after she starts going to the gym again, after she decides to give in to a bit of First Month Nausea . . . the man often invites her for lunch. He may even propose.

SLUG IT OUT.

10

Too Much, Too Little, Too Late

When an unmarried keen woman is going to a wedding with Him she feels a bit nervy.

She doesn't know whether going to the wedding will help him to 'get the idea' or precipitate a Panic Attack.

She is unsure whether to try to catch his eye during the vows. She decides against and leaves her hand dangling at her side instead. In case he wants to give it a little squeeze.

She figures that 'catching the bouquet' would definitely be a bad idea and goes to the loo during the throwing. In case he thinks she was trying to catch it.

On the way home she is very sweet and tries not to talk too much about the proceedings. In case he DID 'get the idea' and is thinking about it.

The man wonders whether he's missed the start of The Match.

Sometimes a man will propose to a woman way before Slug It Out rears its ugly head. Sometimes a man will propose during Phase Three. A Phase Three proposal is usually bred in one of the following circumstances.

- The man is already married to someone else.
- The woman is already married to someone else.
- The woman is about to leave the country.
- All of the above.

A Phase Three proposal is generally of the passionate variety. Often both the man and the woman are at least partially disrobed when the proposal occurs. It is the kind where the man's mouth is very close to the woman's ear and he suddenly hears himself say 'Marry me'. They are both a bit stunned. A lot of kissing and mumbling ensues.

If a Phase Three proposal is discussed over breakfast it may lead to marriage. However, a woman in these circumstances likes to clarify a few details. She starts talking about lawyers, living arrangements, timing and general difficulties. The man starts to feel quite relieved that she didn't say, simply, 'Oh yes, Darling.'

The woman doesn't say simply 'Oh yes, Darling', because:

1   At heart, she is not the romantic creature she imagines herself to be. At heart she is a practical little body.
2   A woman expects that a Passionate Proposal will be followed up by a Proper Proposal.

The Proper Proposal

Proper Proposals occur after. . .

a)   the divorce papers come through
b)   she gets back from Australia
c)   a few months of 'going public'.

Proper Proposals are the kind which involve quite a lot of fore-thought by the man. Men who decide to go for the Proper Proposal option can be amazingly inventive in terms of romantic planning. A really Proper Proposal includes A RING.

Actually, it is a well-kept secret that men love shopping for an engagement ring.

This is because:

1 Men enjoy spending serious money once THEY have decided to do it.
2 Men think that producing an engagement ring under the right circumstances will prove how romantic they REALLY are.
3 Men think that they have fabulous taste in women's clothes and jewellery.

When the Proper Proposal happens (usually after a great deal of subterfuge which has left the woman feeling a bit irritated), the woman has several conflicting emotions:

1 She is still a bit irritated.
2 She is thrilled and feels terribly guilty about having been irritated with him EVER.
3 She wants to TELL someone.
4 She doesn't like the ring.

When a woman doesn't like the ring her thoughts go like this:

'Ooooh. . . has he NEVER noticed that I ONLY wear white gold? I don't believe it. How can I tell him? I'll bet he took that naff tart from the office with him to choose it. It's just the sort of thing she'd go for. Well, I mean I simply CAN'T wear it.'

This is one of the happiest moments of her life.

> Very Occasionally some poor fellow spectacularly misjudges a Proper Proposal and is met by a rather distressed but nevertheless unequivocal NO. This is the stuff of tragedy and alcoholism.
>
> More often the woman goes along with the idea for a bit – 'It's always nice to be asked' – and an eleventh-hour Broken Engagement drama is played out instead.

The What the Hell Proposal

This is a modern variant. This kind happens when the couple have been living like man and wife for some time. They may have played Slug It Out for a bit but then they just settled into an 'Understanding'. This kind, typically, occurs one weekday evening at their flat. The woman is generally engaged in some sort of humdrum domestic activity which the man feels

a) familiar with
b) comforted by.

He suddenly finds himself moved to go up and put his arms around her, restrain her from chopping any more carrots and propose.

The Postpartum Proposal

The man. . .
Acts a bit funny during the starter. Thinks she looks fabulous. Thinks, 'She didn't look this fabulous when she lived with me . . . did she?'

Mutters something about good times. Mutters something about understanding each other. Mutters something about marriage.

The woman. . .
Acts pretty cool during the starter. Thinks he's looking a bit rough. Thinks, 'He looked a lot better when he lived with me.'

Thinks, 'Good Grief, he's trying to propose.'
Thinks about it.

Some Men Play Proposal Roulette
These guys propose on the second date. They say things like 'You know I might even ask you to marry me one day.' They propose to women who they suspect do not fancy them one bit. They propose to pretty girls in wine bars. They propose to the receptionist every morning.

This game can be thrilling but the players generally come to a sticky end.

POST PROPOSAL PRE-WEDDING PLANNING

The woman. . .
- Starts telling people at the first opportunity
- Asks HIM who he has told.
- Thinks about THE FROCK.
- Discusses THE FROCK with her friends.
- Tells her friends she wants something a bit different.
- Looks vaguely at a few things that are a bit different.
- Tries on a traditional white wedding dress.
- Decides she wants a traditional white wedding dress.
- Tells her friends that HE would like her to have a traditional white wedding dress.
- Thinks about WHERE. WHEN. WHO.
- Asks HIM what he thinks about where, when and who.
- Doesn't wait for an answer.
- Discusses every wedding she has ever been to with her friends.
- Decides that her wedding will not be like any wedding she has ever been to.
- Doesn't bother to tell HIM this.
- Possibly argues with her Mother about it.
- Orders the invitations.
- Starts writing invitations.
- Leaves a few invitations and a carefully written list for HIM to start writing.
- Has a fight with him when he doesn't do it.

The man. . .
- Genuinely cannot understand what all the bloody fuss is about.

Wedding Planning Variations

Low-key weddings. These are planned and executed with the minimum of fuss. In a low key wedding

The woman. . .	*The man. . .*
Buys something to wear.	Shows up.
Buys him something to wear.	
Books the registry office.	
Books the restaurant. Writes	
out the invitations herself.	

> Elopements and secret weddings are most likely to occur after a What the Hell Proposal. The couple go to great lengths to organize it themselves and the planning is mutual. The man doesn't tell anyone. The woman ONLY tells...

11

Just Say No

Girl-Talking Some More

'So anyway, he took Charlotte out for dinner and told her that he still loves her.'

'Uh huh.'

'Like, he got really upset and said that, you know, even though he's engaged to this other woman, Charlotte is still The One.'

'Right.'

'I mean, it just goes to show.'

'Uh huh . . . what?'

'Well, this other woman. She's only known the guy three months and she's already got a ring on her finger.'

Forty-five-minute analysis follows.

....

Not all women want to get married. Quite a lot of women do not want to marry the man that they marry.

Generally these women go ahead and do it anyway.

Reasons That Women Go Ahead and Do It Anyway:

- Single women are invited to girls' nights and 'just us' evenings.
- Single women over twenty-five only get to go to swinging parties and swanky dinners if someone can 'find them a partner'.

- Single women who love their cats are objects of pity.
- Single women get hit on by married men.
- Single women are always wondering whether to give First Month Nausea another bash.
- Single women are constantly being asked if they would like to marry and have children ONE day.

If a woman has 'a' man people ask her if she is going to marry him.

If a woman has two men people wonder when she's going to get 'a' man.

If a woman has more than two men people think she's a bit of a slut.

All this is very confusing. The woman can opt for 'no men' or 'secret affairs' but then people think she is LONELY or a LESBIAN.

She is confused as to why she cares about people thinking either of these things.

It's a minefield.

That is why a woman can find herself swept up in the nuptial wave before she's had a chance to say 'Let me think about it.'

Sometimes a woman does say 'Let me think about it.'
Men who are faced with this response usually persist.

A bachelor is pretty convinced that most women would like to marry.

He is even more convinced that most women would like to marry him.

The woman thinks about it for a bit.

Quite often a woman hasn't given marriage any particular thought. She meets a man and rather likes him. Things go along smoothly for a while and then, one Sunday morning, the man says: 'Look, I think it's only fair to tell you that, you know, marriage really isn't on the cards for me. I'm just not into marrying ANYBODY.'

When the man says this, something strange happens. The woman does NOT burst into peals of laughter and say: 'Actually I don't remember asking you.' Instead she says: 'Oh . . . no . . . right. Of course not,' and she thinks: 'Why did he say that? Why wouldn't he want to marry me? I mean I MIGHT want to marry him. Not now exactly but SOME day . . . maybe. Maybe he's thinking that too. Maybe that's why he mentioned it.'

She thinks about it for a bit.

A man does not realize that by saying something like this he is not 'getting himself off the hook'.

He is, in fact, 'throwing down the gauntlet'.

Sometimes a woman has been with a man for quite a while. This man has asked her to marry him, in a casual, over the shoulder, testing the water kind of way. The woman has thought about it for a bit. She finds, though, that she is thinking more and more seriously about a nice little garden flat and a kitten.

One day, she is passing the estate agent's in the High Street and she pops in. She tells the agent what she is looking for. The agent cannot decide whether to laugh or simply look at her with disdain. Sometimes the agent does both. If this incident coincides with a birthday which begins with a 'three' the woman quite often goes home and thinks about marriage for a bit.

Rough Guide

Reasons a Man Gives For Not Marrying a Woman
- He is at a crucial stage in his career.
- He doesn't want children.
- He is broke.
- He is rich.
- He thinks he is too young.
- He thinks he is too old.
- He doesn't want to be monogamous.
- He likes being on his own.

Reasons a Woman Gives For Not Marrying a Man
- She is not 'in love'. (She still thinks about it for a bit.)

Given that the single life can be wearing, given that a man will persist when he is told NO, given that two can live cheaper than one, given that men get to do the asking . . . a woman is usually tempted.

She often succumbs.

As soon as the proposal is accepted, the woman who has acquiesced is outwardly indistinguishable from the woman who has insisted.

12

Honeymoons and Hiccups

And Then Some. . .

'So we're eating breakfast and he says, "There's something I want to tell you," and I'm thinking . . . well, you know . . . anyway, he says, "I'm getting married," and I say "When?" and he says, "Thursday" . . . can you believe that? . . . Bastard!'

'Bastard!'

Thoughtful pause.

'He hasn't called.'

'Bastard.'

Forty-five-minute analysis ensues.

Honeymoons used to be the other thing (besides Proper Proposals) that men got to flex their romance muscles on. The man used to be able to spring it on her post-reception. The woman would just have to behave and accept his non-committal answers to her giggly 'give me a hint' queries until then. She would smile and say gushily to her friends, 'He says I'm to have a cholera shot AND pack a fur coat!'

The thing is that nobody wears fur coats any more.

These days the couple do the honeymoon together. It is a reflection of the fact that they are equal partners. This means that the woman makes a few suggestions after a trip to the travel agent's and the man has the power of veto.

Usually. . .
- Women like to go somewhere hot where there is nothing to do.
- Men like to go somewhere not too hot where there is plenty to do.

They compromise.

As a rule they go somewhere extremely hot with water sports or somewhere freezing with churches.

TRAVEL AGENTS KNOW THIS

Extremely hot means two weeks but no one can stomach freezing churches for more than five days. Anyway, if they do go for freezing with churches the couple generally plan on two sweltering weeks of water sports a bit later on.

TRAVEL AGENTS KNOW THIS.

Even though the chap doesn't get to play mystery honeymoons any more, he usually manages to pull off one pretty decent stunt at some point during it.

Pretty Decent Stunts That Chaps Pull Off

- Having the honeymoon suite decked out with roses.
- Having a present delivered with a card that says 'To the Beautiful Mrs. . . '
- Going down on one knee in the street and 'proposing' all over again.

When they get back from the honeymoon a woman likes to tell her friends about this. She does not tell her friends that they had a bloody row on the third day.

What Couples Have Bloody Rows About on the Third Day of their Honeymoon

- How to get back to the hotel from the Église of the Sacred Heart.
- Going to the Église of the Sacred Heart in the first place.
- How to pronounce *prosciutto*.
- Some slag in a lime green bikini.
- Some absolute ponce in a lime green G-string.
- Windsurfing.

The couple get over this row pretty quick and in general everything is hunky dory. This is partly because the man is feeling happy and relaxed.

WHAT HAPPENS WHEN A CHAP ASKS A WOMAN TO MARRY HIM

Before a man proposes, he is vaguely aware that he is holding all the cards. Afterwards, he is absolutely astonished at how quickly control is wrested from him.

A man does connect a *proposal* with *marriage*, but he is rarely prepared for the speed with which this becomes an inevitability.

Many a fellow proposes in May with the vague notion of marrying next summer, only to find himself firmly at the altar on September fifteenth.

Having worked himself up to the great proposing feat, having done what he was SUPPOSED to do, the man would quite like to rest on his laurels for a spell. Instead, he has a period of minor irritation because he is constantly being asked to do things that he can't see the necessity for BUT this wears off. Lots of other fellows give him a pat on the back and girls kiss him and people buy him drinks. The man finds himself settling into the idea. Many a man has a last minute naughty flirtation but this is just wild oats. In fact, he may not even remember the incident.

Once a man is married he feels in charge again. He also feels the weight of decision-making lifted from him.

He is capable of being a very GOOD boy indeed.

When the couple first get back from their honeymoon they feel very in love and together. So they argue constantly.

These are NOT rows. They are just silly fights. They are about rules, roles and territory.

Mostly the woman starts them. A newly married woman is capable of being a very BAD girl indeed.

It's Like This. . .
When a woman accepts a proposal she gets very busy. Everyone knows that a wedding, no matter how low key, is about THE BRIDE. Even if she opts for a minimum trimmings ceremony, any woman who is having a wedding and a honeymoon has got a few things to do. At the very least, there are the outfits (the DAY, the Day before, the Day after, twelve co-ordinating honeymoon).

After the Wedding and the Honeymoon she is not quite so busy.

One day, after they've been home for a few weeks, the woman stops by the dry cleaner's after work. She needs to pick up her Fairy Princess dress from the 'Specialist Service'. She goes home and hangs the Fairy Princess dress in the back of the wardrobe. It is still wrapped in plastic. She has to squish it in a bit because of the engagement party frock and the co-ordinating honeymoon things.

She takes her shoes off and goes down to the kitchen. She puts the groceries away. She turns the grill on and coats the chicken breasts with ready-made marinade.

While she is doing this she notices something that she has been vaguely aware of ever since she did the honeymoon laundry. It is a feeling. She feels this feeling in the same place as she used to feel the Insecurity Alien. She knows that it is NOT the Insecurity Alien. It is Nothing. It is a little void. A hollow feeling. Deep, deep inside her.

The man comes in and gives her a kiss.

The woman shrugs, just slightly. Smiles a half smile. Sighs, and puts the chicken breasts under the grill.

The man is unsure how to proceed. He says: 'Everything OK?'

The woman says . . . 'Fine.'

FINE is a loaded word when a woman uses it solo.

If a woman says 'Fine' with no back-up, she means that everything is as far from OK as it could possibly be.

The man has already weathered a few silly fights about 'Thank You Notes' and his best friend's drinking habits so he recognizes the tone if not the code word. He goes into the other room and reads his paper with the TV on.

The woman feels the void.

When the chicken is ready, the woman calls the man. The man pours them a glass of wine and they sit down.

They begin a fairly innocuous conversation but the woman can STILL feel the void so, after a while, she says something about HIS FAMILY.

His Family . . .

Before the wedding the woman tends to see His Family as key allies. However, this relationship often erodes rapidly after the nuptials. The woman speeds this process along by making niggly remarks about them as often as possible.

The man doesn't notice this for a bit. When he does he tries to ignore it.

This particular evening, though, he is a bit tired. He is a bit fed up. He is mildly irritated that she didn't give him a proper kiss. He reacts. His reaction is swift, sharp and decisive.

This man has PUT HIS FOOT DOWN.

The woman feels a little Thrill Chill run down her spine and fill up the void. She backs off.

They finish their supper.

13

Annus Quite Nice

....

A man NEVER refers to a woman's ex by name. If it is absolutely
necessary that he refers to the guy at all, he will 'forget' his name or use
some vaguely derogatory generalization to do with his job or nationality.

....

The woman knows that the Thrill Chill game is dangerous. That's
why she likes it. That's why it is so effective in filling the void.
Nevertheless, she doesn't push it.

In between times life goes along like this:

The woman. . .
Does most of the housework.
Pays her half of holidays and
treats. Saves up for his
Christmas present. Buys the
groceries. Cleans the loo.
Watches James Bond videos
with him. Watches car racing
with him. Nags a bit. Drops off
his dry-cleaning. Calls the Gas
Board. Waits for the man from
the Gas Board. Buys a duvet
cover for the spare room. Buys
a Le Creuset frying pan. Does
most of the cooking. Nags a bit.

The man. . .
Cooks spag bol, occasionally.
Agrees to go to a Merchant
Ivory film, once in a blue
moon. Wonders what to do
with his bonus.

The man finds all this very comforting. He is very happy.

Secret

There are not many creatures on earth who are happier than a newly married man. Given that men rarely marry unless work is going OK and money is going OK and life generally is going OK, the newly married man often feels that he is Lord Of All He Surveys.

He likes this feeling. He rather likes Putting His Foot Down too.

The woman is very happy as well. She tells her friends that she is very happy. It's just . . . something.

The woman would like a bit more division between how things were BEFORE and how they are NOW. She would like to feel a bit more Married. She'd like to do something that married people do. She doesn't know what this is.

> One way for married people to figure out what other married people do is to do lots of things with other married people.

Something that married people like to do together is to have a barbecue.

HAVING A BARBECUE

The women. . .

Go to the supermarket. Buy the meat. Make salads. Buy bread. Ask each other if they should buy bread or make salads. Put crisps and nuts in baskets. Put all the glasses on a table in the garden. Move all the glasses to a bench in the kitchen. Put the baskets of crisps and nuts on the table in the garden. Joke about how the men will probably make a hash of lighting the barbecue.

The men...
Make a hash of lighting the barbecue. Eat all the crisps and nuts in the baskets. Ask the women to put some glasses on a table in the garden.

When very sophisticated married people have a barbecue the men don't make such a hash of lighting it. The women put small foreign things in wooden bowls instead of crisps and nuts. They have grilled peppers and olive oil instead of salad. And they invite *someone* who is not married. (Preferably someone artistic, homosexual or both.)

Afterwards, when the woman has finished putting the baskets (or wooden bowls) in the cupboard above the fridge, she knows that the barbecue wasn't it. She can still feel the void.

During the first year or two of their marriage the woman is in constant search of void fillers.
These are some of the things she tries:

- Having a chair re-covered with fabric from Colefax and Fowler.
- Buying all the things that nobody got them off the 'wedding list'.
- Getting some cushions that match the re-covered chair.
- Figuring out ways of having her Fairy Princess dress turned into something that she can 'wear again'.
- Trying out some different ready-made marinades.
- Getting a new Hobby or Interest.

73

Occasionally a woman turns her void filling talents on to her husband. The woman thinks that it would be nice for HIM to have a Hobby or Interest. (She thinks how this would solve the Christmas present problem, too.) This tack can backfire badly on a woman. Sometimes a husband will take to a hobby like a duck to water. Particularly if it is a hobby which can be pursued in an attic, garage, shed or 200 miles down the M4.

The woman's void problem gets even worse.

She just cannot figure out what is wrong with her. She Has It All. Good job. Nice Husband. Own Home. Pre-booked Summer Holiday.

She thinks vague thoughts of babies. She thinks No. Not yet. She's not ready to give up Pre-booked Summer Holidays.

What IS it?

One day the woman stops on the way home and buys a magazine. The magazine has an article in it called 'The Love Workout'. The woman turns her attention to this article as soon as she's read the horoscopes. The Love Workout informs her that modern relationships are NOT about frothy nightgowns and home-made shepherd's pie. The woman thinks 'That's for sure.' The Love Workout says that modern women have got their hands full with their careers. 'True,' thinks the woman. Modern relationships are Equal Partnerships says The Love Workout.

'UH-huh. . . ' thinks the woman. Modern relationships are about COMMUNICATION.

Bingo.

'That's IT,' thinks the woman. 'We've been so busy with the house and organizing the holiday and having people over that we haven't really TALKED. Not for ages. . . '

Now, a woman is not a fool. A woman waits. A woman with something like this on her mind goes home and quite possibly makes home-made shepherd's pie and puts on a frothy night-gown. (Modern equivalent: fresh pasta and shortie 'black thing'.) Much later, when the man is feeling completely content and happy with his lot and kind of sleepy from the effects of the fresh pasta and shortie black thing, the woman says:

'Let's talk.'

When a man hears these two words he is at a loss to explain the unnerving effect that they have on him.

He hesitates for a moment and then he says: 'Mmmm. Let's get some sleep, huh.'

He is then able to induce an instant coma-like condition complete with deep sleep sound FX.

The woman lies awake for a bit. She feels the void. She thinks: 'I wonder if those curtains would look nice in the same fabric as that chair.'

14

Oh Baby

Some women belong to the 'I've Experienced Childbirth' Club.
These women KNOW that no one else has Experienced Childbirth
quite like they have.

They like to point this out to their STILL single friends and to men.

With their STILL single friends they adopt a 'just you wait',
tolerant kind of a tone.

With men they adopt a 'Women are SO amazing and capable and
Men are SO pathetic and useless' tone.

In between graphic descriptions which involve the words 'bricks'
and 'sideways' they complain a lot about how little their men do for
them.

Often, one of the reasons that a man eventually puts a ring on a
woman's finger is that he would quite like some kids.

Often, the woman would quite like this too but sometimes she
hesitates at the last hurdle.

When a man is getting keen on baby-making he surprises
everyone by buying some spectacular, expensive and totally
inappropriate gift for his godson, who he has previously ignored.

A woman faced with a man clutching £200-worth of remote
control equipment is sometimes so touched by his beaming smile
that she feels a bit broody herself.

When the woman gets pregnant, she keeps quiet about it at first. She certainly doesn't let on at work. She feels very tired and a bit confused. She pees a lot and she discovers that the smell of Pizza Florentina makes her want to die. She still keeps quiet about it.

One day her sister comes over for a cup of coffee. The woman pees three times in an hour and then she bursts into tears and TELLS. She feels better after that.

The man is very tender and considerate throughout this process and he only ever orders Four Seasons. He is glad when she tells her sister.

Eventually they go public with the pregnancy. Everyone is very happy for them.

They are VERY happy.

The woman notices that the void has gone.

She thinks, 'That must have been IT.'

She stops saying 'Let's Talk'. In fact she talks less. She goes into a little imaginary baby world at every opportunity. Sometimes she is a bit tired and weepy. Sometimes she worries about the enormity of it all. She worries about something being WRONG.

The man is very reassuring. He is happy to talk about the baby. For once he is happy to talk about the future.

They have lovely conversations late at night about why they are not going to call the baby Sebastiano after all.

It is a magical time. They feel very important.

When the woman goes into labour the man feels very UNIMPORTANT for a while. But once the baby is born, he swells right up again.

77

The man goes on feeling important for about twenty-five minutes.

When a man and a woman create a child they are pretty amazed at themselves.

The man tends to be a tiny bit more amazed at himself than the woman is.

They are both amazed by the child. They both worry.

The woman tends to worry a tiny bit more than the man does.

The modern man says. . .
'This is the most incredible thing that has ever happened to me. Having a child has brought everything in my life into focus. I am SO conscious of the fact that I have to BE there for this little person. It has totally changed my life.'

The man's life is totally changed for about twenty-five minutes.

The modern woman says. . .
'We are determined that having a child is NOT going to change our lives.'

The woman's life is totally changed. For ever.

Modern women have the choice of staying at home with their babies or going back to work. The modern woman who has been buying the groceries and paying her half of treats and holidays does not have to be very good at maths to figure out what will happen if she stays at home.

After a brief spell in miracle land, many a modern woman drags out a suit that still fits her and gets on with it.

The woman then begins a period in her life which involves so much hard work and so little sleep that, years later, she will wonder how she survived it. (Women who don't go back to work are sometimes able to delay the onset of 'Absolute Exhaustion' until they have a second baby.)

Things That Women Suffering From 'Absolute Exhaustion' Do

- Let their hair go back to its natural colour.
- Have another drink.
- Wear the same clothes every Saturday.
- Have another bread roll.
- Buy a lot of Fish Fingers.
- Wear the same clothes every Sunday.

Things That Men Do When Their Wives Are Suffering From 'Absolute Exhaustion'

- Take the kids to the park on Saturday mornings while she has a sleep in.

The man quite enjoys taking the kids to the park.

The man considers himself a much better Father than his Father was because he kisses his son and knows his daughter's reading age.

The man thinks of himself as an 'involved' parent.

The man is sympathetic about his wife's 'Absolute Exhaustion'. He doesn't mention anything about her hair and he sometimes pours her another drink.

It's just . . . something. A feeling.

A feeling that he isn't Lord Of All He Surveys any more.

He has a sneaking suspicion that other people might be a tiny bit more important than he is.

The man feels a void.

One evening Karen from Accounts stops by his desk at six o'clock. She says that she is leaving and a few of them are going for a drink after work. She says it would be nice if he could come. Just for an hour or so.

Karen's hair is a rather unnatural colour.

15

Home Is Where the Heart Is

Men tell women that they look better with no lipstick on and then go and flirt with some tart wearing half a ton of slap.
  This Really Pisses Women Off.

When a man has had a drink with Karen from Accounts, and one thing has led to another, and something that he hasn't planned has just happened, he gets home a bit later than he said he would.

The man does a guilty creep into the bedroom and he sees his Absolutely Exhausted wife sleeping soundly. She has her natural-coloured hair spread out on the pillow. The man looks in on his baby on the way to the bathroom. He runs the shower on full pressure for several minutes. Then he does a guilty clamber into bed.

The woman half hears him come in. When he gets into bed she gives him a little cuddle. She does not notice the time. She does not notice that he has wet hair.

The man has two thoughts:

1 He has behaved like a Complete Bastard.
2 He seems to have gotten away with it.

In the morning the AE woman is quite jolly. She shows him the birthday party invitations she wrote out last night. They agree that they are very cute. She chatters idly about the possibility of a barbecue on Saturday. She smiles at him as she eats the left-over mashed banana.

Eating the Left-over Mashed Banana

This requires no crockery or cutlery. It is a reflex action. The right hand simply conveys the food to the mouth as the plate is being moved from baby chair to sink. Speech is not interrupted.

The same method is used for: lemon curd triangles, mini pizza wedges, fish fingers, marmite soldiers and animal biscuits.

The man has two thoughts:

1 He has behaved like a Complete Bastard.
2 He has definitely gotten away with it.

Why a Man With an AE Wife Can 'Get Away With It'

The AE wife is often very happy. Despite her AE condition. She has no voids. She can hardly remember what an Insecurity Alien is. She is much too busy to SNOOP.

In fact, the AE wife would forget about Insecurity Aliens and SNOOPING altogether except for her STILL single friend, who comes over occasionally when the husband is out at 'some pre-arranged work thing'.

When the AE wife notices that the STILL single friend seems to be having a 'bad patch', she swallows a bit of fish finger and says: 'Honestly, hon, don't worry. Look at me. *I* used to be JUST like that.'

She says this with a little reminiscent smile. Then she swallows a bit of banana and says: 'I was always crying over some Complete Bastard.'

They both have a jolly good laugh at this.

The AE wife's laugh is a bit jollier.

The AE wife doesn't worry about losing the 'couple cocoon' any more.

The AE wife considers that she lives in a 'couple fortress'.

The ideal couple fortress is twenty-four bus stops from the centre of town. It has a garden for barbecues and 'the kids'. A lot of small, hard things are on the floor. The walls are covered with Blu-tack and a variety of misshapen coloured objects hang from the ceiling.

When the AE wife's husband brings home some flowers for her, she is almost overwhelmed with happiness. She has tears in her eyes. She hugs him. She kisses her child and thinks:

'I am SO lucky. EVERYTHING is SO perfect.'

The husband who has behaved like a Complete Bastard does his best to blot the incident from his mind because (and Let's Get This Clear) he LOVES his family. He would do NOTHING to hurt them.

The one-time CB husband mends his ways pretty damn quick. He pulls his socks right up and behaves like a VERY good boy for quite a while.

The one-time CB husband is particularly attentive to his children.

As AE wife watches him stop fiddling with the barbecue in order to gently demonstrate the mechanics of some small, hard thing to their son, her heart swells. She thinks again how Perfect everything is. Everything, that is, EXCEPT. . .

There is one blot on the landscape of the lovely life of the AE wife.

The Nanny.

When the AE wife first gets the nanny, she says:

'I can't believe how lucky we were to FIND her. Honestly, Maxie just ADORES her. She is a GODSEND.'

It is not long before the AE wife discovers that the nanny is, in fact, an Evil Witch Woman from Hell who is likely at any moment to perpetrate one of the following crimes:

- Get lipstick on the Colefax and Fowler chair.
- Steal the car.
- Steal the car and the children and kill them all in a hideous wreck.
- Drink all the coffee.
- Telephone Australia.

The AE wife is on to this though, and she wages a serious campaign to keep control of the situation. She leaves NOTES.

She is pretty sure that she can stop things from getting too out of hand this way and she knows, after all, that SHE is the Queen of the Couple Fortress.

The REAL problem is that her husband is not terribly sympathetic.

It doesn't matter how BADLY the nanny behaves or how vividly the woman describes this behaviour to her husband, she is unable to get him to UNDERSTAND.

This niggles her.

One night they go out for a Moroccan meal. The nanny baby-sits. The man is as unreceptive as ever to the woman's (perfectly justified) nanny complaints, but they have a nice evening anyway. A nice comfortable sort of evening. They are back by ten-thirty. When they get home, the nanny's friend Susi is there.

The woman sees her husband smile and say something to the two girls. She hears them all laugh. She realizes that she hasn't seen her husband (or any other man) smile and laugh quite like that for a very long time.

Later, she shuts the bathroom door and looks at herself in the full-length mirror. She sees a lot of fish fingers, banana, lemon curd triangles and mini pizza wedges looking back at her.

She has two choices. One of them is to have another drink.

16

Shape Up Ship Out

A man loves it when a woman gets all dolled up to go out with him.

A man hates it when a woman spends ages getting all dolled up to go out with him.

If an AE wife decides that having another drink is not the answer, she wakes up the morning after the full-length mirror incident with a GOAL.

The man doesn't notice that she has grapefruit and black coffee for breakfast. He doesn't notice that she keeps doing this. He pays no attention at all when he sees her rummaging for her aerobics gear. It irritates him slightly that the scales are always in the middle of the bathroom floor.

He is vaguely aware that she has stopped complaining so much about the nanny.

One day the woman goes to the hairdresser's and gets her hair dyed back to its unnatural colour. She buys a new suit. When she slides the skirt over her new hip bones she feels pretty good about herself.

That night her husband asks her if she'd like another drink. She says, 'No thanks.'

He looks up at her . . . he *keeps* looking. He goes up behind her and he puts his arms around her new waist. He gives her a little nuzzle at the place where her new hair is tucked behind her ear.

She smiles.

He suggests an early night.

Later on, when the man is aware that all is right with his world, he takes a big breath and steels himself. He decides to talk about his FEELINGS. This is what he says:

'You are an absolutely wonderful Wife and Mother.'

He says some other stuff too. It is the kind of stuff that the absolutely wonderful wife and mother has wanted him to say for a very long time. She doesn't know why she doesn't feel QUITE as happy as she thought she would when he does say it. She gives him a hug and says:

'Mmmm. Let's get some sleep, huh.'

After this, the woman gets used to her new waist, hips and hair. She feels assured of her husband's devotion. She begins to carry herself with a certain confidence. One day a chap in the marketing department says to her: 'I'd like to discuss this stuff with you, but I'm pushed for time. Would you mind staying on a bit late this evening? We could go over it together.'

No modern chap would ever say anything as crass as 'and there's a few other things I'd like to go over too. . . ' but when he looks up and smiles at her the woman can see a hint of this in his eyes.

Her stomach contracts.

It is one thing to have a new waist, it is quite another to have someone look at you as if you were NOT an absolutely wonderful wife and mother.

The absolutely wonderful wife and mother has two choices:

1   She can go home to a land where people love her and need her and there is always the sound of cartoon characters singing.
2   She can sit in an office with an attractive man, eat Chinese food and play the Thrill Chill game very seriously indeed.

Whichever of these choices the woman makes she will resent her husband for it . . . just a tiny bit.

Things That a Woman Does When She Resents Her Husband . . . Just a Tiny Bit

- Looks gorgeous.
- When her husband tells her that she looks gorgeous she gives him a sort of 'Like YOU'D notice' look.
- Buys new clothes.
- Accuses her husband of not noticing this.
- Accuses her husband of being penny-pinching if he *does* notice.
- Says 'I am NOT your housekeeper.'
- Feeds him very badly and DARES him to mention it.
- Feeds the children very badly and DARES him to mention it.
- 'Forgets' that his squash partner and his wife are coming over for a barbecue. Feeds them very badly and DARES anyone to mention it.

The man. . .
Feels a bit baffled. Keeps his head down. Feels a bit hurt. Buys pizza. Feels a bit confused. Takes the kids for a pizza. Starts to feel really pissed off. PUTS HIS FOOT DOWN.

When the man puts his foot down:
The woman looks up at him and starts to shout. She accuses him of EVERYTHING he has EVER done to hurt, humiliate or anger her. She goes WAY back. She drags out Insecurity Aliens and

SNOOP evidence from years ago. She hits him with the time the kids had measles. She slugs him with the First Birthday when she wrote all the invitations by herself. She dredges up years of mashing bananas and cooking his favourite suppers. She even alludes to a Karen from Accounts type incident, even though she knows nothing about it. She just lets him have it.

Eventually she bursts into tears. She sits on the sofa. She shudders with great racking sobs.

The man is stunned. He is unable to speak. He doesn't know where to start.

Nothing is right with his world.

After this, one of two things happens:

a) The woman asks him to move out of the couple fortress. She begins to communicate with him through her lawyer. He gets a lot of bills for new clothes and pizza.
b) They have a cautious hug and another drink.

17

Flings and Roundabouts

Men like women to watch them play sport. The less the woman knows about a particular sport the more the man likes her to watch him play it.

Before a couple are married the woman goes along with this. She buys clothes especially for 'watching him play sport in' and she keeps a lipstick and a comb in her pocket at all times. She combs her hair and reapplies her lipstick in a hideous institutional loo where there is a cracked mirror and no loo paper. She doesn't care. She's with HIM. On the way home (after His side get creamed), she listens attentively to his lengthy and defiant protests about the ref and the other side.

After a couple marry, the woman cannot imagine anything more gruesome than 'watching him play sport'. She does everything she can to get out of it. If a man is foolish enough to INSIST that his Wife should come and watch him play sport he doesn't understand why she looks miserable and cold during the match and then spends the whole drive home pointing out to him that they got creamed.

Sometimes a man who is keen to recapture the rapture of the early days will suggest (in a casual sort of way) to Karen in Accounts that she might enjoy the inter-departmental play-offs.

Karen goes out and buys an angora sweater and a strawberry chapstick.

Sometimes a man's Complete Bastard behaviour extends way beyond the Karen from Accounts incident.

Sometimes a woman looks at herself in a full-length mirror and sees fish fingers and lemon curd looking back at her and she doesn't care.

She thinks: 'Who'd want to be twenty-two again and have to put up with First Month Nausea?'

She thinks that it might be nice to have another baby or another dog or another house.

This woman goes into the bedroom and ribs her husband a bit about flirting with the nanny's friend and then she gets into bed and gives him a cuddle.

It is very cosy indeed.

Women who get used to dealing with kids and dogs develop a few habits that they find useful for keeping things running smoothly:

- They talk rather loudly so that kids and dogs can hear them.
- They wear clothes that will resist kids and dogs.
- They talk to Everyone as if they were a kid or a dog.

The husband of a woman who behaves like this has two choices.

a) Allow himself to be treated as if he were a kid or a dog and become passionate about his Hobby.
b) Misbehave and become passionate about his Hobby.

At first this man is very cautious about misbehaving, but one day he and his wife and the kids and the dog go somewhere for a barbecue.

Someone's teenage daughter is at the barbecue with one of her friends. The man flirts a bit in a 'silly old goatish' kind of way with these girls. His wife passes by. She calls him a 'silly old goat' and wipes some spilt food off his tie.

After that the man is pretty open. The man has A Mistress. The wife finds out about the mistress. She refers to her as 'That Woman'.

Under these circumstances the wife either. . .
Leaves the man, spends all his money, mocks his hobby and becomes very bitter and unhappy OR she Sticks It Out: this means that she doesn't leave him. Instead, she spends all his money, mocks his hobby and becomes very bitter and unhappy.

IF the woman leaves the man he generally likes to marry again and get a few more kids and dogs as soon as possible.

Sometimes a woman feels much better after she has got a few things off her chest. She bucks up her ideas and starts feeding everyone properly again. Maybe she doesn't look gorgeous twenty-four hours a day but she doesn't look half bad. She is a wonderful Wife and Mother. One day, while she is waiting for the gas man, she decides to get the man's blue suit out. She intends to drop it off at the dry cleaner's. When she is clearing out the pockets she finds a card with the message 'I Love You Too' written on it. The woman makes a phone call to the lodge where her husband was 'fishing' last weekend.

Her world falls apart.

NB When the recipient of the 'I Love You Too' card is confronted with this card by his wife HE LIES. He *keeps lying* until it is absolutely apparent that there is no point in lying any more.

THEN HE SAYS: 'I didn't plan this. It Just Happened.'

> Sometimes a girl just goes ahead and marries herself a Thrillseeker. Typically, this girl 'Waited'. Typically, this girl wheedled, cajoled, pleaded and Slugged It Out. This girl is SUSPICIOUS from day one. But she REALLY believes he is REFORMED when the kids come along.
>
> She gives him a bit of rope. She gets Herpes.

In order for men to behave like Complete Bastards there have to be women who are prepared to play the game. . .

The Bored Wife

The bored wife doesn't stray far. She prefers a tumble with her husband's best friend or someone she works with. She feels very guilty. She dreads HIM finding out BUT then she falls in LOVE and wants them to 'bring it all out in the open'.

The man is likely to call it off. Quick Smart.

The Transitional Girl

This girl has an eye for men who are about to make an exit. She can spot a restless husband from the other side of a smoke-filled room. She feels a bit guilty – about the kids – BUT then she falls in LOVE and wants them to 'bring it all out in the open' so that the kids can stay with them on weekends.

The man is likely to call it off. Quick Smart.

The Other Woman

This woman falls in LOVE straight off. She feels a bit guilty about the wife but she knows that this is THE REAL THING. This woman plays hard. When the wife finds her 'I Love You Too' card she is both thrilled and terrified. She thinks: 'At least it's all out in the open now.'

If the wife forgives the man he is likely to call it off. Quick Smart.

The Mistress

Never feels particularly guilty because it has always been pretty much 'out in the open'. Gets over being in LOVE quick smart. Knows that the man is unlikely ever to call it off.

The Slag in a Lime Green Bikini

Just wants to have fun. She never feels guilty about not mentioning her herpes.

18

Never On a Sunday

'So what's the problem with this woman then?'

'Well, she just gets so hysterical, makes scenes, you know, and cries all the time.'

'Right. So . . . gonna ditch her then?'

'Can't . . . she'd get hysterical, make a scene and start crying all the time.'

'Right.'

There are lots of women who get to have a nice sleep in on a Sunday, go to the gym straight after their cappuccino and see every episode of the Sunday Night Period Serial on the TV.

These women are Bits On The Side.

BOTS are distinguishable from Mistresses because they are less cynical and they have less money. BOTS might have some jolly nice clothes, but they certainly don't have a fur coat.

BOTS are distinguishable from Other Women because they are much more discreet and they try hard to be sensible about being in LOVE. BOTS are essentially part-timers.

It is not only married men who have them. Often men who have a full-timer like to get one. Or a chap may just have a whole series of BOTS for a bit.

BOTS do *not* think that All Men are Complete Bastards.

BOTS think that, actually, SOME women are Witches who are out to destroy men and that men might be a bit Misunderstood.

A BOT spends quite a bit of her time trying to Understand why the man she is seeing behaves suspiciously like a Complete Bastard.

A BOT does not discuss this with the other girls. A BOT knows she risks a lecture about 'where she stands' if she discusses this with the other girls, so she just talks to her cat about it.

If she doesn't have a cat any passing cat will do.

A man genuinely likes his BOT.

A man may toy with the idea of turning a BOT into a full-timer on account of liking her so much. But he doesn't do this.

This is because BOTS don't really play the game.

A man is a bit confused because a BOT avoids crying in front of him. (She does this on Sunday Nights during the sad bits in the period serial. If there are no sad bits a slushy bit will do.)

A BOT doesn't nag and she tries hard to be cool about the full-timer and the other BOTS. Sometimes she is even sympathetic towards the full-timer.

This can make a man very uneasy indeed.

If a BOT stays over at a man's house she can be relied upon *not* to Leave Something Behind.

Leaving Something Behind

If a man is quite keen on a woman, or even just vaguely keen, he sometimes leaves something at her house.

This thing will be Obvious and Distinctly Masculine. The woman will have noticed it before the man is out the door. She will do one of these things with The Thing:

a) Keep it lying about so that other girls can see it and she can see it whenever she is feeling slushy.
b) Chuck it, as soon as his car is out of sight.
c) Send it back at an awkward moment.

When a woman leaves something behind at a man's house she doesn't leave something obvious. A woman who wants to mark a man out for her own knows that, as soon as she leaves, he is going to do a quick 'lacy knickers under the bed inspection'. A woman is smart. She leaves something accidental behind. This Thing is vaguely scientific and, therefore, easily overlooked by a chap who is on the hunt for something that he considers 'girlie' and a 'giveaway'. He *never* notices a tube of tinted moisturiser tucked between the Savlon and the Colgate, and a half bottle of nail polish remover can go undetected for months.

BOTS, though, don't do any of this stuff and that means that there are never any Scenes with the man.

A man who never has any Scenes with a woman is not likely to make too many moves one way or another so a BOT finds herself just going along with the man for a good long time. A BOT never knows where she stands.

The BOT wouldn't mind this. She wouldn't mind it at all if someone, somewhere, would just hand her a stone tablet with these words on it:

'You will not wake up alone on your fortieth birthday.'

A BOT does not want to spend her fortieth birthday with Hercule Poirot.

Birthdays and Public Holidays are the natural enemies of BOTS and Other Women.

Other Women can usually be relied upon to make a Scene on these occasions and a man who is involved with an Other Woman has probably painted himself into a corner with a pretty heavy whitewash of lies before the Date actually arrives. As D-Day draws near, he will find himself increasingly caught up in conversations which seem to require specific commitments from him.

Specific Commitments are the natural enemies of men.

BOTS handle these situations differently.

A BOT tends to try to forget about Birthdays and Public Holidays all together. In fact, except for sleeping in and going to the gym, a BOT wouldn't mind much if every day were a work day.

When the Birthday or the Public Holiday does arrive and the man she is seeing has not been forced by a Scene to make any Specific Commitment to Do anything about it, a BOT feels a bit depressed. The man she is seeing feels like a bit of a heel.

On her birthday the BOT does one of the following:

a) Cries a bit and eats too much pasta in front of the TV.
b) Goes out and eats too much pasta with another BOT.
c) Eats too much pasta at the home of some married friends.

If a BOT has really had it with the Pasta Eating Scenario . . . if a BOT begins to suspect that men are Not so Misunderstood after all . . . if a BOT feels a Scene coming on . . . she may just call her ex.

An ex is always pleased to hear from a woman. He is flattered. He is secretly pleased that she has turned to Him on her birthday. The ex tells a bit of a whitewash story to his full-timer or his own BOT and he takes the woman to 'their' restaurant.

A woman doesn't always catch on that he considers this to be 'his' restaurant.

A BOT who is spending her birthday with her ex is liable to drink too much red wine with her pasta. The red wine intake and a lot of suppressed Sunday Night emotion starts to build up during the evening until, suddenly, the BOT astonishes the man, the two adjoining tables and herself by Making a Scene.

This Scene is likely to be a real Humdinger. The BOT figures she has nothing to lose. She gives the ex a right ear-full. Hits him with a detailed, blow-by-blow inventory of the faults of the man she is currently seeing. (These faults are attributed to Men generally.)

The man looks over the table at her. Her cheeks are flushed from the red wine. Her eyes are flashing. She looks all fiery with passion.

The man feels compelled to do something.

He reaches for her hand (to the detriment of the pepper grinder).

He gazes lovingly and sympathetically at her.

The woman takes a slow sip of her wine and stops ranting. She looks over at her ex, all sympathetic and loving. She does a mental check list of his faults and those of the man she is currently seeing.

Depending on her exact level of red wine consumption one of three things happens:

a) She starts to feel all slushy about her ex. This lasts until the following morning when he says something intensely irritating.
b) She starts to feel all slushy about the man she is currently seeing. This lasts until the following Tuesday when he hasn't called her for a bit.
c) Hercule Poirot starts to look like a Dream Date.

19

Parting Shot

A man says:

Why can't a woman be more like a man? Why are all women so Bossy and Needy and OBSESSIVE?

Eventually this man meets a woman who is funny and sexy. She is Independent and Cool. She seems totally uninterested in the state of his sock drawer and she NEVER reminds him about anything.

After a bit the man has a thought. (He knows this is silly.) He thinks: 'Maybe she doesn't REALLY love me.'

This man is apt to go out and get himself a bit of crying on the side.

When a woman Acquiesces she often says 'yes' to a Nice Guy. This is usually because she has had a good run of Complete Bastards.

On their wedding day she looks more like an Ice Queen than a Fairy Princess and the man looks like a boy who has caught a butterfly in a jar.

The Acquiescent Woman does not want to move into a Couple Fortress. She likes as much contact with the outside world as possible.

The Acquiescent woman is positively nauseated by the sight of an AE wife.

The Nice Guy is very tolerant. He never does anything as Neanderthal as PUTTING HIS FOOT DOWN.

Their lives go along like this:

The man. . .
Does his share of the housework. Pays for most of the
holidays and treats. Saves up
for her Christmas present. Buys
the groceries. Cleans the loo
occasionally. Never watches
James Bond videos. Asks if she
minds if he watches car racing.
Suggests a Merchant Ivory film
on Sunday evenings. Drops her
dry-cleaning off with his. Irons
his own shirts. Stays in to wait
for the man from the Gas
Board. Talks about his feelings.
Buys a Le Creuset frying pan in
a sale because he knows they
need one.

The woman. . .
Leaves him.

The Nice Guy is the ONLY member of the male sex who ever
gets to wake up with a note.

After a woman leaves a Nice Guy, she sighs and says to her
friends, 'The thing is that, you know . . . he really is *such* a Nice
Guy. . .'

This type of behaviour tends to make ex-husbands rather bitter.

The woman's problem is that she plays Slug It Out and Insecurity
Aliens for so long that when she stops she thinks she mustn't be
IN LOVE any more.

101

After she leaves a Nice Guy the Acquiescent Woman often goes and plays at 'Other' Woman for a bit. Just to get back to the edge.

Men say: 'Women only like Complete Bastards.'
This isn't true. Women like 'Rough Diamonds'.

A woman likes to think that a man is a Nice Guy struggling to get out of a bit of a Complete Bastard. If she can help him to do this it will prove that he never met the right woman before.
She likes to do some polishing.

Women always smile when people say, 'He has really settled down since you two got together.'
Women say: 'Honestly, he's so HOPELESS,' and laugh.

> When a couple split up a woman is often annoyed because she considers that she has done some 'groundwork' for the next woman.

A Nice Guy is no use to her because he tries not to rely on her. A Nice Guy doesn't need any work.

Sometimes a woman flys the coop because she wakes up one morning with a keen desire to 'make her mark'. Her exit is swift.
About a year later she and her cat have a few blue evenings in front of the TV. This is because they've realized that a new-look hairdo, a new-look wardrobe and a diploma in Interior Decorating isn't IT.
Quite often this woman meets a Rough Diamond, devotes three months to completely redecorating his flat and then spends a good long time waiting around for him to show his gratitude.

This type of behaviour tends to make ex-husbands rather bitter.

When women decide that they need to 'find themselves' they very rarely find themselves on a Greek island with Tom Conti.

They are more likely to find themselves in a draughty school-room at eight o'clock on a Tuesday night listening to some plonker drone on about Spanish vocab.

If the plonker has two legs, a penis and only very mild halito-sis . . . if the woman is REALLY desperate to find herself . . . she may become convinced that he IS Tom Conti.

Sometimes she can go on with this delusion for a good long time.

This type of behaviour tends to make ex-husbands rather bitter.

A bitter ex-husband often meets a Nice Girl.

He is a bit suspicious of this girl because he is pretty sure by now that all women are Witches out to DESTROY men and that they only like Complete Bastards.

He tells her this.

The woman who hears this feels all her tingly bits come alive.

The woman who hears this NEVER sympathizes with the ex-wife.

The woman who hears this KNOWS that this man has 'Never met the right woman before'.

20

Chequing Out

A man who is misbehaving is quite likely to throw a jealous wobbly when His woman shows any interest in another man. This applies to both the full-timer and the Bit On The Side.

This can throw women off the scent for a bit.

The man doesn't realize this. He thinks it was the carnations.

A man doesn't leave his wife to find himself. He never lost himself. A man only leaves his wife if he falls in love with the Other Woman.

The man usually thinks about this for a very long time. He knows that this type of exit can prove to be a very expensive proposition.

When a man does finally leave his wife, he just goes on being himself with the new woman. He takes her to the same restaurants and gives her the same sorts of flowers.

This type of behaviour tends to make ex-wives rather bitter.

> If a man gets into bed with a woman, rubs her left titty three times, kisses her ear lobe and then strokes her hair, it is a pretty safe bet that he has been using this little magic cocktail since he was about twenty-one and hasn't had any complaints so far.

By the time a man leaves home he is often a fairly unhappy boy.
He has had months, maybe years, of strain. He's been getting a
load of 'what's going on?' earache at home and a load of 'where
do I stand?' earache elsewhere.

Nobody really Understands this. NOBODY seems to be able to
see it from HIS point of view. Not even the Other Woman. Who
he is in love with. Well, she has pretty much convinced him that
he is, and he figures he *must* be since he seems to have screwed
up his entire life on account of her.

The man doesn't tell the Other Woman that there *was* a point
where he'd have happily ditched her in a caddish jiffy if his wife
had only been able to see reason.

In fact, he'd been thinking vaguely of ditching her ever since
the first 'where do I stand?' conversation. But then he got rumbled.

A man is never quite sure how it is that he 'got rumbled'.

The man doesn't realize that one night he got into bed with his
wife (feeling a bit exhausted from all this stress), and proceeded
to rub her *right* titty and stroke her hair simultaneously. No ear
lobe at all.

At that moment his wife did a swift mental inventory of:

- odd phone calls
- 'pre-arranged work things'
- suggested visits to her Mother's.

She IMMEDIATELY developed a sudden, urgent need to take a
few suits to the dry cleaner's.

After the 'I Love You Too' card nightmare, the man has a really
terrible time. His wife turns into a Witch who is out to DESTROY
him and the Other Woman is HAPPY! What's more, she expects
HIM to be happy because it is 'all out in the open'.

This man really doesn't understand women at all. He is also likely to find himself living in Severely Reduced Circumstances. He sees his Net Worth shrinking by the minute. He is NOT Lord Of All He Surveys.

The Other Woman simply cannot figure out what has gotten into him. OK, so her flat is a bit poky, but it's THEIRS now and she's got a camp bed for the kids. That is, once his Witch of a wife sees reason and lets the kids come for the weekend.

The Other Woman is FULL of plans. She tries to tell the man about them but all he wants to do these days is stare at the TV and drink out of cans.

One Saturday morning the man has to go over to 'The House' to get something. The Other Woman does not like this idea ONE BIT. She is very specific with him about what time he is going to get back. She makes PLANS and tells him about them so that he has no excuse to linger.

She is thrilled when his car pulls up in the driveway only forty-five minutes after he leaves. Sweet relief. She thinks: 'Everything will be fine now. He's over it. We can make some plans.'

She busies herself in the kitchen so as to appear casual. When she hears him open the door she calls out: 'All right, Darling?' in a very sweet way.

She is absolutely stunned when the man comes crashing into the kitchen with a face like thunder and SHOUTS: 'There's some plonker with halitosis in MY house, wearing MY dressing gown!!'

When the Other Woman hears this she is extremely upset. She conceives twin Insecurity Aliens. She starts crying a lot.

This is the last straw for the man. He has to get out for a bit. He takes the car.

The woman cries and cries. She is really HURT. It wasn't meant to be like this. All those months of waiting, pleading, whining and cajoling. All those months of not knowing 'where she stood'. All her PLANS.

After a while, the man comes back. He is still pretty grumpy but he has reverted to merely morose. He switches the TV on, he gets up to get a can out of the fridge. He hears her crying. Something about this sound pierces his melancholy. He feels like a bit of a heel. He goes into the bedroom.

The Other Woman looks all small and vulnerable. She looks like a funny, fuzzy ball of Love actually. He feels a bit sorry.

The man goes over to the woman and puts his arms around her. She continues to make little whimpering noises. The man wishes she wouldn't, he gives her a wee pat. She keeps making those little noises. He says: 'Come on, love,' and pats her again.

She looks up at him. Her eyes are all glisteny from crying. The man thinks: 'She must REALLY love me.'

He thinks: 'Maybe I'm better off, after all, without that Witch, she was probably ALWAYS out to Destroy me and she obviously prefers Complete Bastards anyway . . . THAT plonker!'

The man smiles at the woman. He kisses her head.

The woman feels all relieved and in LOVE. She rests her head on his shoulder.

The man sighs and makes a vague move for her left titty.

The woman doesn't discourage this so he heads for the ear lobe.

Just then. . .

The woman looks up all HAPPY and suggests that they go away to some remote beach on the other side of the bloody world and stay in some million-pound-a-minute exclusive resort.

The man feels a vice close round his heart.

At that moment he KNOWS that ALL women are Witches who are out to DESTROY him.

21

Play It Again

If a man has had an affair, a woman insists that he never sees or has anything to do with That Woman again. She manages to exact a promise to this effect from him.

She then proceeds to bring up The Affair and That Woman at every opportunity. Men can't Understand this.

If a man has an affair and leaves, the woman says that the past twenty years and their children meant NOTHING. She really believes this. Men can't Understand it.

If the woman has an affair and the man says 'We'll never mention it again', the woman leaves him.

One day a Ditched Wife wakes up with the awful realization that the man next to her is a plonker with halitosis. She realizes that learning Spanish isn't IT. She realizes she is still a Ditched Wife.

She has a little weep. If the plonker tries to comfort her he finds himself in the street pretty smartish wearing nothing but the Errant Husband's dressing gown.

(This is generally enough to convince him that women are Witches who only go for Complete Bastards.)

One day an Errant Husband wakes up with the awful realization that he is not, and probably never was, in Love with the Other Woman. When the Other Woman wakes up and sees him packing he tells her this. It only takes two sentences.

The Other Woman becomes hysterical. But the man figures that being blunt will make it easier for her to get over him. He may point out to her that it's all been a terrible, terrible mistake. (He does this because he doesn't like hurting people.) The Other Woman becomes suicidal. The man leaves.

(The Other Woman is convinced from here on in that ALL MEN ARE COMPLETE BASTARDS.)

The man rents himself a bijou apartment, suitable for his Reduced Circumstances. It has a TV though, and a fridge, and the man feels a bit better about everything. He puts the snapshot of his wife (the one that the Other Woman made him take out of his wallet) on the table next to the bed.

After he has put his socks away and moved the TV to a different corner the man feels that he is Lord Of All He Surveys. He hasn't felt like this for a very long time. He picks up the phone and calls his wife.

He tells his wife that he has moved.

His wife thinks: 'Oh my God. He's left that slag. Well, he needn't think he's walking back in here just like that. He needn't think that I'm going to LET him. . .'

She says: 'Uh-huh.'

The man says that he needs a few things for his bijou apartment and would she mind very much if he took some of the stuff in the cellar.

The wife thinks: 'This place must be an absolute hovel. I can JUST imagine.'

She says: 'Actually, I've got to go out later, so if you tell me what you need I could pop it in to you.'

She says this in a very casual, take it or leave it kind of tone so as to make it clear that she is NOT eaten up with curiosity.

The man says: 'Uh-huh.'

He thinks: 'I'll bet she's just eaten up with curiosity.'

They come to an arrangement. Six o'clock, or thereabouts . . . they are both pretty busy, after all.

The woman. . .	*The man. . .*
Gets the things out of the cellar. Puts them in the car. Takes a shower. Washes her hair. Thinks about what to wear. Tries on clothes until she hits on a combination which looks as if she just threw it on but might be on her way to somewhere quite nice. Does her make-up. Is ready to leave at five o'clock. Waits. She doesn't want to be early.	Buys a bottle of wine and puts it in the fridge.

When the woman rings his doorbell her heart skips a little beat.

After they have brought the things in from the car there is an awkward silence.

The woman looks at her watch.

The man says: 'Got time for a glass of wine?' He wants to make it clear that he has all the home comforts.

The woman says: 'Well. . . ' She wants to make it clear she has got things to do. 'A quick one, I guess. I said I'd meet some people. . . '

The man says: 'The schoolteacher?'

The woman says: 'Spanish LECTURER, actually! . . . but no, as a matter of fact. . . '

The man feels his Lord Of All He Surveys mood coming on again. He goes and gets the wine.

The woman says that she needs to wash her hands on account of bringing the things in from the car. The man directs her to the bathroom. She has to go through the bedroom to get to it. On the way back she notices her snapshot lying on the bedside table. She feels a tug in her tummy. She feels a lump in her throat.

Much later, after they have drunk the wine and the woman has explained that she DID say to the others that she MIGHT NOT be able to make it, they decide to get a take-away pizza.

They sit on the sofa and eat the pizza. One of them suddenly remembers the thing that made them laugh so much that they had to leave the restaurant all those years ago. They laugh and laugh.

They laugh until the woman starts crying.

The man puts his arms around her and holds her very tight. After a bit he takes her chin in his hand and tilts her face up to him. He looks into her eyes, all glisteny with tears.

She looks into his eyes and she thinks that they look a bit glisteny with tears.

They both think: 'We'll just see how things go.'

22

Sweet Harmony

One night when the woman is getting ready for bed she says, 'Look at me. I'm so fat. I must have put on two stone.'

The man keeps reading.

The woman says, 'LOOK.' She clutches two handfuls of orange peel-like substance at an awkward angle at the back of her thighs and waggles them.

The man thinks fast. He knows that he is in a minefield. He says:

'Sweetie, even if you weighed twenty stone I'd still love you. Come and have a cuddle.'

He smiles.

He considers that he has cleverly diffused the situation.

The woman is upset.

The right answer is: 'No you haven't. The scales must be wrong.'

He should be prepared to say this at least three times. The woman will then go on a diet and lose two stone.

The first answer is likely to convince her that he doesn't CARE.

She just might gain another two stone.

> Some people grow up in houses where grown-ups dance in the kitchen.
>
> Some people grow up dreaming of houses where grown-ups dance in the kitchen.

If a man and a woman who come from houses like this or a man and a woman who dream dreams like this get together they can often weather lots of storms.

This man and woman come to love each other very much. They are Best Friends.

The woman says: 'You know, we are not IN LOVE any more. I don't think that I ever want to be IN LOVE again. We have something more than that. Something much DEEPER somehow. Something much more INTIMATE.'
   The man: Would never dream of saying ANYTHING like this. Cannot imagine life without her.

When this man and woman sort out their Rules and Roles they understand an awful lot about each other. There are some things they Never Understand. . .

One Sunday morning the man is treating himself to a nice long soak in the bath. He notices that there is only a small bit of soap in the dish so he reaches up and takes some soap off a shelf nearby. This soap is kind of a yellow colour and it is shaped like a shell. It is a tiny bit dusty.

The woman comes into the bathroom. She says something cute to him and laughs, but then her expression changes.

She says: 'Why did you use THAT soap? There's *plenty* of soap in the cupboard.'

The man can see from her expression that she really is a bit upset.

There are two things that the man does not understand:

1   Why would you have soap on a shelf if you're not going to use it?
2   What is the Difference between the soap on the shelf and the soap in the cupboard?

The next day the man stops by a chemist in the High Street. He buys some soap. It is lime green and shaped like a tree. He is Trying.

When he hands her this soap she laughs like a drain and gives him a smooch.

He doesn't really understand.

One afternoon the man notices that something has fallen down behind some shelves. He carefully removes the ornaments and knick-knacks on the shelves in order to rescue the thing. He puts all the ornaments and knick-knacks back EXACTLY where they were.

The woman comes into the room and IMMEDIATELY moves each of the ornaments and knick-knacks by a quarter of an inch.

The man cannot understand this.

The woman cannot understand why he can never put things back how they were, 'on an angle'.

One evening the woman says to the man: 'I think I'll wear that green dress of mine to the party.'

The man says: 'Uh-huh.'

The woman says: 'I KNOW you don't like it, but I really haven't got anything else.'

The man cannot remember what the green dress looks like.

He cannot understand why she thinks he doesn't like it.

He cannot understand how she can say she hasn't got anything else.

The woman cannot understand why he says he likes it when she KNOWS he doesn't.

The woman never understands why the man won't ask for directions.

It seems strange to her that he will not answer a perfectly simple question when he is driving.

She wonders why he doesn't just 'SAY so'.

The man can't figure out why the woman never realizes HOW sick he is.

He doesn't know what she wants to talk on the phone about.

It is a mystery to him that she could possibly doubt that he loves her.

Nothing that a smooch and a dance in the kitchen won't fix.

In a Great Love

A man and a woman are always Completely Honest whenever they tell each other anything.

They would never dream of telling each other EVERYTHING.